Also by Mollie Bartelt

A Simple Guide to Saving Your Family Photos

Amazon Reviews from "A Simple Guide to Saving Your Family Photos"

I recently finished reading this book and cannot recommend it highly enough. This is a step-by-step guide to organizing your physical photos in a very clear, easy to read book. Not only does she explain the process but gives specific examples to further illustrate how it can be done. You can read it cover to cover for or refer to it later for examples of how to organize your photos using different methods. This is a great guide for a person needing to tackle years of photos or needing to update their collection. Please read this before you start!

C. Burnham, Professional Organizer

The step-by-step guidelines provided in this book are clearly thought out and you can tell is based on the author's experience of doing lots of photo organizing. Having made a couple of attempts to organize my family's photos I identify with why Bartelt doesn't call the process easy. However, after reading through this guide I definitely feel like I now have a simple road map to follow that can finally get me on my way to getting my photo organizing project completed.

Rick Lippert, E-Z Photo Scan

Library of Congress Control Number: 2017937210

Printed in the United States of America

First Printing, 2017

ISBN: 978-0-9978136-4-7

A Simple Guide to

Tackling Your Digital Photo Mess

Using Windows 10

By Mollie Bartelt

Co-Founder of Pixologie

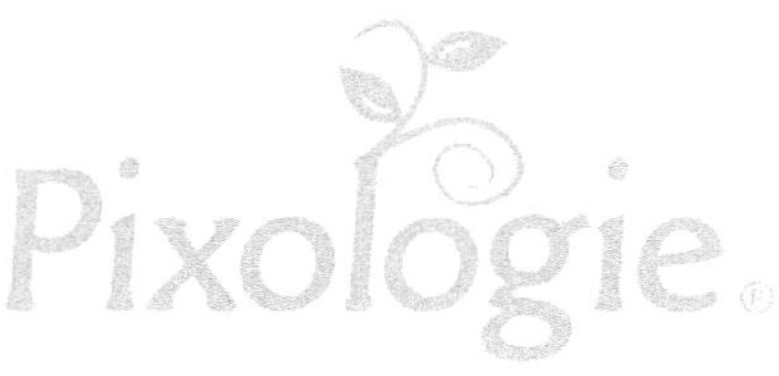

Pixologie . . . the study of life through your photos

TABLE OF CONTENTS

INTRODUCTION

Can you think of anything more easily accumulated than digital photos? And anything more difficult to manage? The number of digital photos can grow like crazy and clog up our phones, computers, devices and so much more.

Have any of these questions crossed your mind:

- Which pictures should I delete from my phone so I have room to take more?
- How do I get those photos out of my email? There are messages back from 2008 that I can't delete because I am saving the photo attached to it.
- How do I print photos from a text message?
- Where are the pictures I saved to my computer with that software I bought I few years ago?

Many people have a digital photo mess. The growth in digital photography over the past 20 years has been a blessing, and a curse. Sure, we can take thousands of photos at no additional cost, but do we take the time to manage all of these photos?

In my work as a professional photo organizer, I have seen some whopper digital photo disasters. In one instance, my client's situation included having over 200,000 family photos on her computer. She had quadruplicate copies of pictures and corrupted files located across three different computer log-ins! It took us over 60 hours to sort that out so she could enjoy her photos again.

When we organize photos on client computers, we see similar situations:

- Pictures in many places on the computer
- Many, many duplicate file folders and photos
- Digital photos that are poor quality or corrupted
- Smartphone photos stored in the cloud, on the phone and sometimes in several places on the computer
- Backups of the photos are nonexistent

Please take my advice:

Start with a system now to ensure your current digital photo mess doesn't morph into a galactic nightmare.

Why is this so important? Because our photos are in danger of being lost. For me, that represents memories being wiped away. Life is very busy. Without photographic proof, I literally wouldn't remember a quarter of the things my family has done together. When we look back through my digital photos, those images help my family remember some of our fun times together.

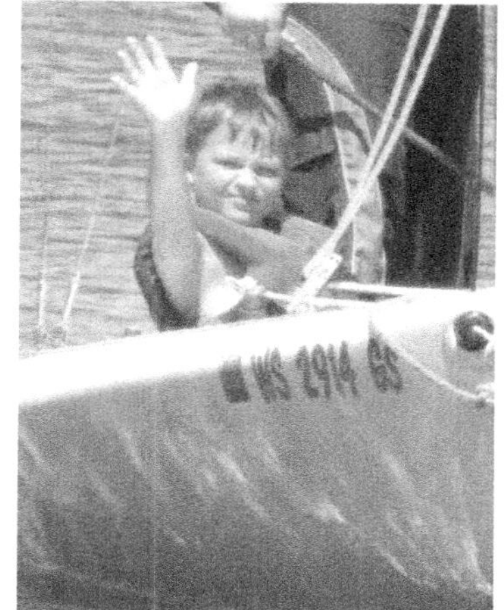

My friend Ann Matuszak and I founded Pixologie, a photo organization company. We are proud to be on the leading edge of finding photo organizing solutions for consumers. At our studio located near Milwaukee, Wisconsin, we have helped hundreds of people figure out what to do with their photos.

Why do so many struggle with making the time to fix their digital photo mess? It should be fun and enjoyable as we reminisce over the events and activities. But many people do not view this task as pleasant. In fact, we have seen people deny they have a photo mess problem. Other people avoid their photo mess because they are overwhelmed. One of my friends has even said she'd rather clean toilets then organize her photos!

Today, Ann and I are making the stand:

Too few people are saving their photos. The day has come to begin as memories are being lost, stories faintly existing and traditions fading away.

Family photos are integral to passing down family values, celebrating the best in life and connecting generations. We have met too many people who know they need to get their photos in order but who do not take action. They feel bad, but they don't see a realistic path to bringing their family pictures together.

How can a realistic path exist when we deal with the countless options of taking, saving and sharing digital photos? Consider the following:

- Many types of devices able to snap a photo (cameras, smartphones, iPads, etc.)
- Hundreds of online providers willing to print, store and share your photos (Walgreens, Shutterfly, etc.)
- Thousands of smartphone apps to help you edit, collage and share your photos
- Many storage options to save and share photos (CDs, DVDs, SD cards, jump drives, external hard drives)

The solution is not in any one of those bullet points. It lies within you. ***To manage your digital photo collection, you need to consistently save your photos in one location.***

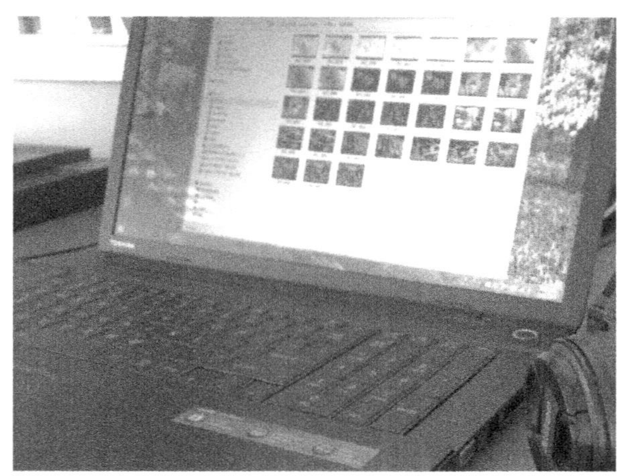

That one location, today, is your computer, preferably, a laptop. This may not be the case in the future. Maybe the cloud will take over, but currently we believe the best home for your digital photo collection is on your computer . . . where you have control and ownership to manage your memories.

Our system, in a nutshell, centers around these steps:

1. Bring all your digital photos to one place, usually in your "Pictures" folder on your computer
2. Save them in folders chronologically using the template YYYY-MM-DD Description for folder names
3. Delete pictures as you go along
4. Back up
5. Repeat (at least monthly)

Pixologie's System of Organizing Digital Photos

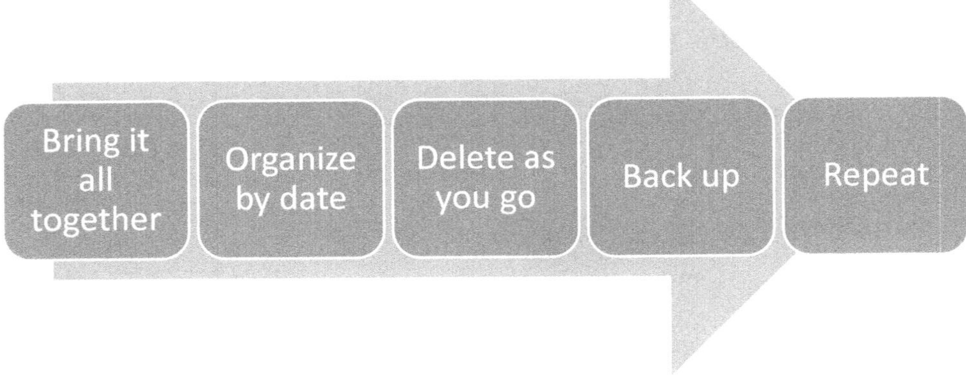

Here's a quick example of how I have saved my digital photos in 2016. Each folder contains the corresponding pictures. Sometimes I just put photos in a folder labeled with the month.

2016-01 Photos
2016-02
2016-03
2016-04 April Photos
2016-04 Concerts
2016-05
2016-05 Alex Concert
2016-05 Hannah Concert
2016-05 Hannah's Confirmation
2016-05 Mission Marcus
2016-06 Crossing the Bridge
2016-06 June Photos
2016-06 Lighthouse Brigade
2016-07 July Photos
2016-07 Lighthouse Brigade
2016-07-03 Alex's BDay Party
2016-07-04 Fireworks
2016-07-09 Trip with Jankes
2016-07-20 Trip to Crystal Lake
2016-08 August Photos
2016-09 September Photos
2016-10 Dells Trip
2016-10 October Photos
2016-10-22 Halloween Party
2016-10-26 Dells Trip

My digital photo collection includes pictures taken with two different smartphones and a camera. In addition, I download photos from email, texts and social media and save them to these folders. It makes no difference what device took the photo; it matters where I save the photos.

You can see I have brought all my photos to one location and organized them chronologically. These photos are saved in my "2016 Photos" folder located within my Pictures folder.

There is more that can be done with saving your digital photos such as tagging, naming and sharing. We will talk about that later in this book. But if you don't start with a basic system, we have seen that it is unlikely you will develop a good habit for the long run.

Besides sharing our simple system for saving your digital photos, we will also discuss:

- How to use your computer to organize photos
- How to get photos off your smartphone, other devices, jump drives, text messages, email and more
- What photos you really need to save
- How to back up your photos

The key to your digital photo organization success is consistency. It is not your computer or software that will determine how well your photos will be saved. Consistency:

- Gives you the ability to frequently repeat the steps you need to do – making them easier to remember
- Provides you the comfort of getting used to deleting photos routinely
- Ensures your photos are saved properly
- Produces results that allow you to look back at a year of photos and to enjoy a curated collection of memories

Photos tell the stories of our lives. We love sharing what we do at Pixologie to help people save their photos. Now that you have opened this book, we hope our system, tips and ideas will help you save the stories of your life!

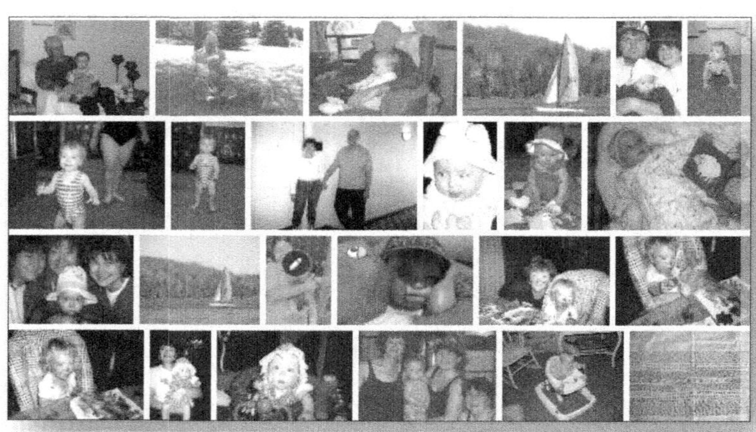

CHAPTER ONE – WHAT DO YOU NEED?

We'd love to tell you that there is an easy solution. The best computer or one program that will make your digital photo organization become the easiest thing on your to-do list. For over 10 years, we've been teaching people how to use computer software for sorting, editing and backing up photos. There is no computer or software that will instantly solve a digital photo mess. It takes time, patience and consistency.

In this chapter, we'll discuss the importance of time and commitment. Then we'll talk about the tools needed to get started.

Time & Commitment

The best solution lies within your ability to take the time and commit to your photos. I can give you the best photo organization system or even software out there, but you need to use it routinely. The benefits of bringing your photos together on a monthly basis include:

- Developing a consistent habit of saving your photos
- Remembering the tricks and tools needed to organize, edit and back up your photos
- Having a system to identify the best photos of the year
- Enjoying your photos and reliving fun moments in life

Ann calls what we do photo life management. It's true – as long as you are taking photos, the photos will need to be managed. Very often, we see people get their digital photos organized for a short period of time. But then as other priorities take precedent, the habit of saving the best photos loses importance. We'll always be able to catch up later, right?

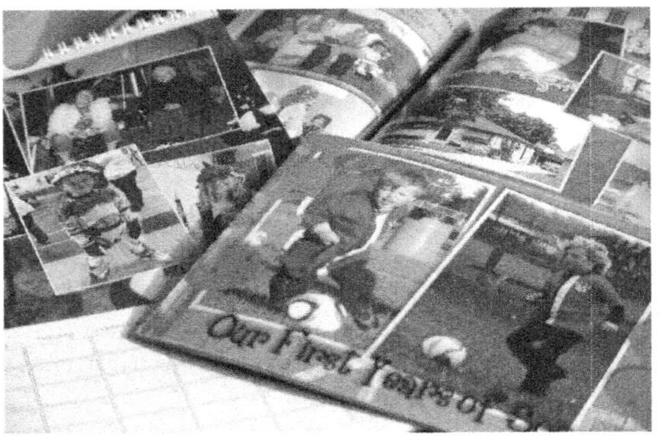

We have found those people who plan year-end projects such as photo books and photo calendars develop the best habits. We'll talk more about that later in Chapter Seven.

When you don't take the time and commit, your photos will continue to haunt you. It may not be a problem today, but it will be when you need the pictures the most:

- To show your son's baby and growing up photos at a wedding reception
- To create a canvas wall print for a quick gift
- To celebrate the life of someone important who has died

The initial organization of your digital photos may take hours, even days. But once you have caught up, maintaining the digital files becomes much easier. Imagine cleaning your home thoroughly over the course of a weekend and then not coming back to clean again until a year later. You'd expect some pretty wild, dirty disasters.

The same is true for your photos. It's a wonderful accomplishment to organize and save your current digital photo collection. Yet if you don't do anything for the next year, you will lose all the momentum you gained. This can lead to further procrastination. When people become overwhelmed by their photo collection, they tend to ignore it completely. Then frustration hits when they need a photo they cannot find. One year of not organizing and saving photos easily turns into three years. That's just how fast time flies!

Working with your photos once a month could take you less than an hour. And, if you are savvy, there are software and apps that automate some of the work for you. But don't assume that automatically uploading and saving pictures means your photos are safe and saved. At Pixologie, we have a strong opinion on this subject.

We consider a photo to be safe or "saved" when the following two conditions are met:

1. ***You can find the photo you want when you want it***
2. ***It is backed up in two locations (one in the home and one outside the home)***

How many of your photos meet these conditions? Time and consistency are needed to keep your digital photo collection in order and safe for the long run.

Let's talk about the tools you'll need.

The Tools for Digital Photo Organization

Since we are working with digital photos, we don't need a lot to get moving on this project. We've mentioned you need a computer already. We love using laptops. You can sort photos and watch your favorite show at the same time!

Here is what you'll need to get started with organizing your digital pictures:

- Your computer
- Any device or storage that contains digital photos
- An external hard drive, possibly two
- Optional - photo organization software

Your computer - Your computer plays an important part as the home of your photos. If possible, we recommend using a computer that is less than three years old. If you are going to purchase a new one, Ann, our computer equipment guru says, *"Buy the computer with the highest amount of storage and memory and the fastest processor that your budget will allow."* If possible, she recommends the following:

- 1 TB of hard drive space
- 8 GB RAM
- 2.4 Ghz processor or faster

If you are using your old computer, that is fine. Make sure it is in good working order and has enough space on it. At Pixologie, we always aim to have at least 25 to 30% of our computer space free. This allows the computer to run faster. When you are dealing with thousands of photos, that extra space can make a difference.

To find out how much space you have on your computer, go to your File Explorer (the folder icon) and right-click on the C: drive. It may have a different word than Windows like mine does in the graphic. When you right-click on the C: drive, a menu will pop up.

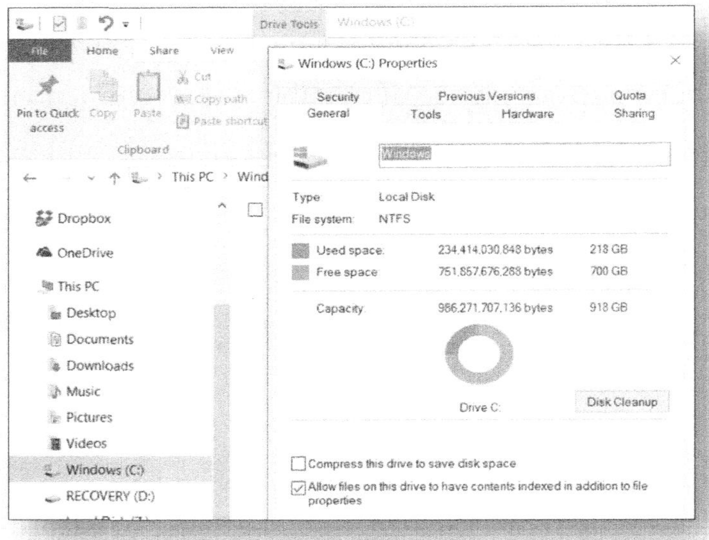

Select Properties. Then you will see a window with your computers properties and available space displayed. My example may look different from yours depending on the version of Windows you have.

If your storage is filled to more than 75%, it may be time to delete some old files. Typically, photos and videos are the largest culprit eating up computer space. Or it may be time to upgrade to a computer with more storage.

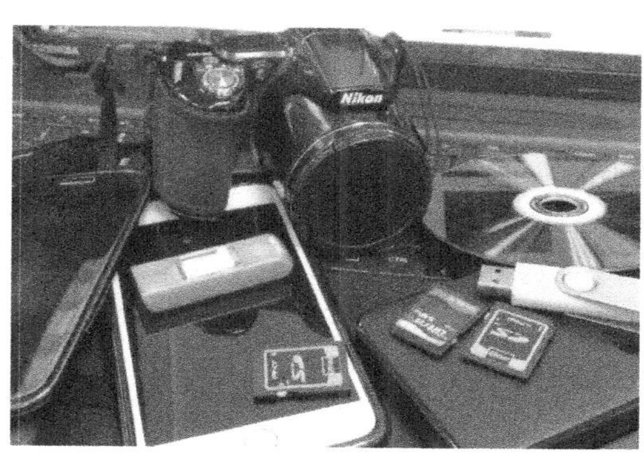

Any device that is storing photos - and appropriate cords to connect to the computer if necessary. Start collecting these items to one location now. They'll be all in one place when you are ready to start. We'll talk about how to get your photos off these devices in Chapter Two. Devices include:

- External hard drives
- USB flash drive/thumb drives/memory sticks
- CDs/DVDs
- Camera cards/sticks
- Floppy disks and Zip drives (yep, we have seen them!)
- Cameras (with photos in memory)
- Smartphones

An external hard drive - Once your digital photos are in your "Pictures" folder, you should back up your photo files to an external hard drive. You may need a second external hard drive to keep a copy of your photos outside your home. If you are planning on using a cloud based backup, then you will only need one external hard drive.

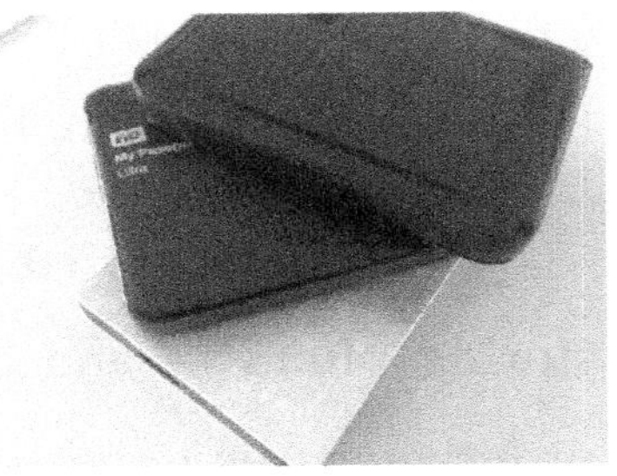

Special note about external hard drives - Some of our clients come into our studio with photo collections stored solely on an external hard drive. By doing this, our client does save space on their computer. We discourage this because external hard drives can:

- Fail
- Accidentally have everything deleted or formatted
- Be dropped
- Be lost or stolen

Photo organizing and editing software (optional) - Your computer comes with everything you need to organize your digital photos. We'll be using Windows File Explorer. Later in the book, I will talk about several photo organization programs you may want to consider. But first, having a basic understanding of how File Explorer works is important. The tips shared will be useful even if you choose to use a specific photo organization software.

Why Use Windows File Explorer?

In this day and age, every day brings forth new app, cloud and software developers. However, there are also app, cloud and software developers who don't make it. Ann and I have seen the effects of several companies who have gone out of business. We are careful about what we recommend. We don't think Windows is going anywhere for a long time!

I teach digital photo organizing classes every month, both at our studio and out in the community. I show the class how to use File Explorer to move pictures around, make new folders and so much more. Many people are not aware of the quick tricks on how to use their PC more efficiently. They love learning the tricks and tips I will be sharing later in this book.

At one of the library classes I was teaching, some people were having a difficult time grasping my Windows basic tips. I paused to reconsider my approach. I wondered if maybe I should be teaching people how to use a specific photo organization software that might be easier to learn. I asked the group "Would you prefer I teach you how to use a single piece of software to manage your photos instead of using what comes on your computer?" Surprisingly, they all agreed they liked learning how to use their computer better!

Having a good understanding of Windows File Explorer is super important to organizing your digital photos. We'll be covering basic tips and tricks along with how to use File Explorer in the next chapter.

CHAPTER TWO – UNDERSTANDING WINDOWS FILE EXPLORER

During our digital photo organization classes, we receive as many questions about how to do things on a computer as we do about which photos to save. In this chapter, we'll show how Windows File Explorer can be used to:

- Move folders and digital files around
- Rename folders and files
- Get basic information about your pictures

For the following examples and screenshots, I will be using the Windows 10 version of File Explorer. A key part of the Windows operating system, File Explorer has been around for decades. In the past, it had fewer bells and whistles and different names (File Manager, Windows Explorer). If you are using Windows 7, see Appendix B for screenshots of Windows Explorer.

Within File Explorer is where we can find our Pictures folder. Possibly, you have a lot of photos in there already. For the next few pages I will be using a "Demo Folder" with a variety of pictures. I will use this folder to show how File Explorer's features can help organize photos in a simple system. You can find the File Explorer icon generally in the bottom menu bar, and it looks like file folders.

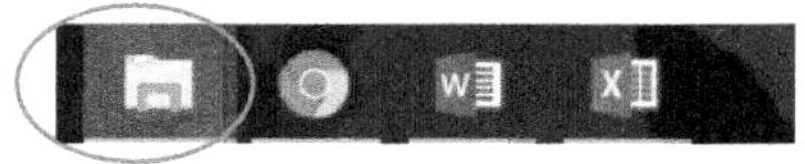

Once you click on that icon, it should open up and give you the following view. Your folder and file names and icons might look different. You should have folders named Documents, Downloads and Pictures visible in the left column, called the Navigation Pane.

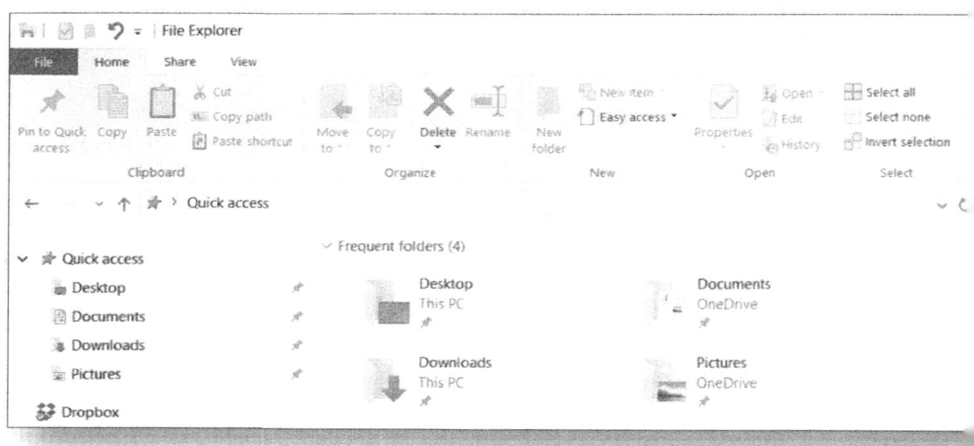

Your photos should be located within your Pictures folder on your computer (especially if you are not using a photo organizing software program). The goal is to move all your photos to the Pictures folder.

Pictures can be viewed in a list or as icons in a variety of sizes. The Detail listing provides us information on when the photo was taken, what size it is and what type of file it is. The Large Icon View gives us a thumbnail view.

DSCN9832.jpg	1/1/2014 12:26 PM	JPG File	847 KB
DSCN9833.jpg	1/1/2014 12:26 PM	JPG File	787 KB
DSCN9834.jpg	1/1/2014 12:26 PM	JPG File	792 KB
DSCN9835.jpg	1/1/2014 12:26 PM	JPG File	809 KB
DSCN9836.jpg	1/1/2014 12:26 PM	JPG File	838 KB
DSCN9837.jpg	1/1/2014 12:26 PM	JPG File	918 KB
DSCN9838.jpg	1/1/2014 12:26 PM	JPG File	911 KB
DSCN9839.jpg	1/1/2014 12:26 PM	JPG File	901 KB

Details View

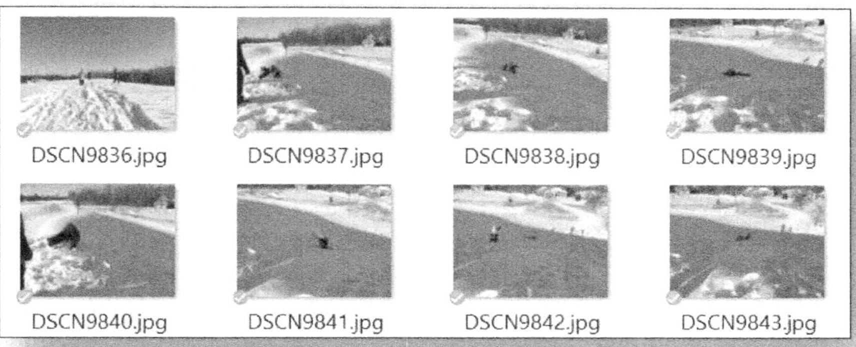

Large Icon View

Over the next few pages, we'll be reviewing the basics about File Explorer with some larger screenshots.

Figure 1 - File Explorer Overview

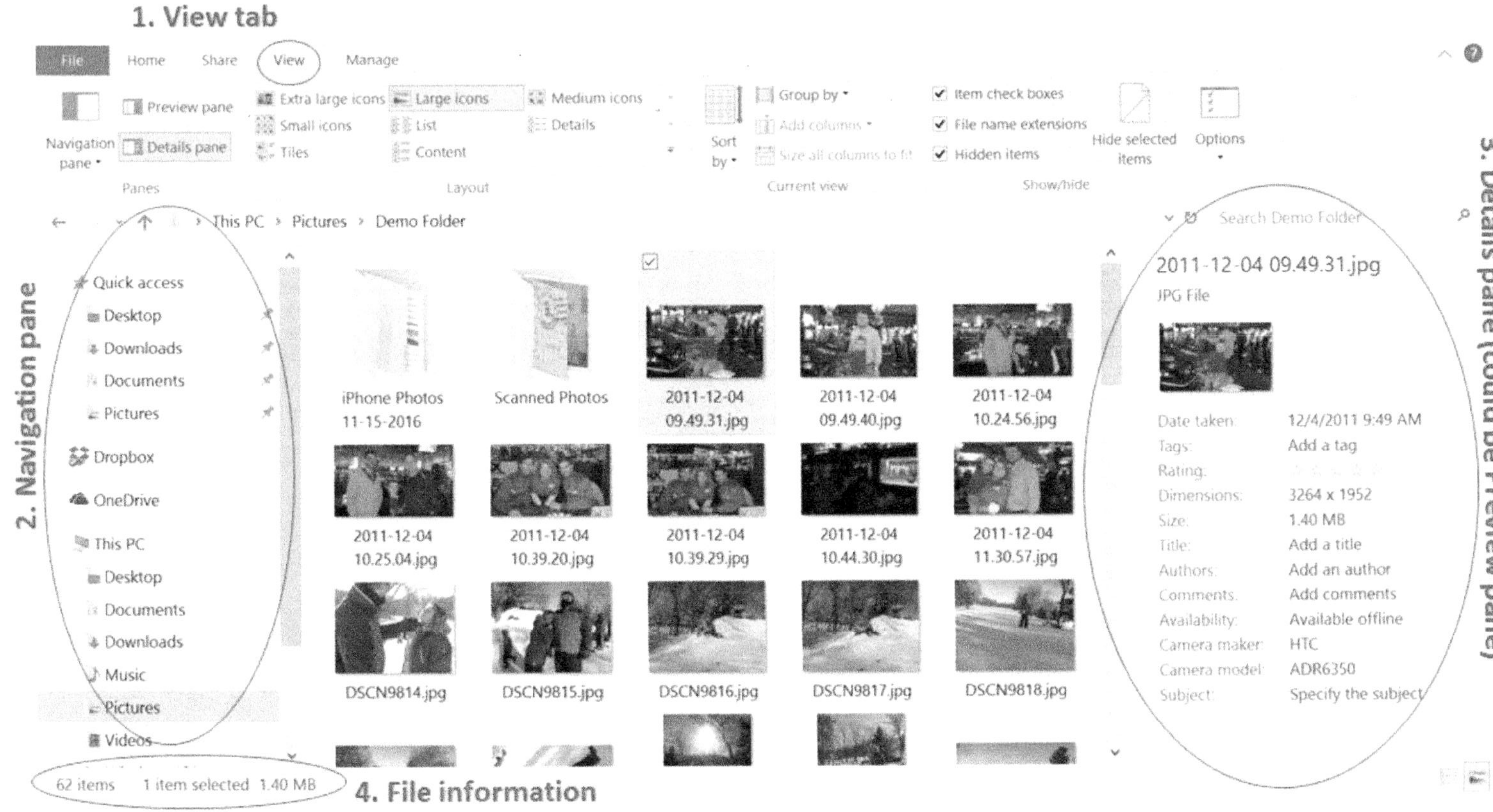

Getting Around in File Explorer

Looking at **FIGURE ONE**, we've circled four areas to provide further information for you.

1. View tab - Change the view of how your photos are displayed (Details, Small Icons, Large Icons, etc.) Adjust which panes (Navigation, Details, Preview) are visible. Sort your photos by name or date.
2. Navigation pane - View the folders on your computer and on devices connected to your computer. (Optional: right-click on the Quick Access area to customize what shows here. Select Options for your choices.)
3. Details pane (or the Preview pane) An amazing amount of information can be found about your photo here when you have the Details pane visible. Don't get caught up in the details, though. Close this pane in the top left of the View Ribbon if you want more space to view your photos.
4. File information - Shows the number of items, how many are selected and the size of the photos.

The more you use these skills with File Explorer, the faster you'll be able to work with your folders and photos.

Now let's look closer at the photos we see in Figure 1. The files are poorly organized. In the screenshot, note the following problems with my digital photos.

- Are the iPhone photos a backup? Or just the photos from November 15, 2016?
- The scanned photos folder – what's in there? When did I last add photos to it?
- Some of my photos have dates. Why do the names have random numbers?
- Looks like I have some similar photos. Do I really need them?

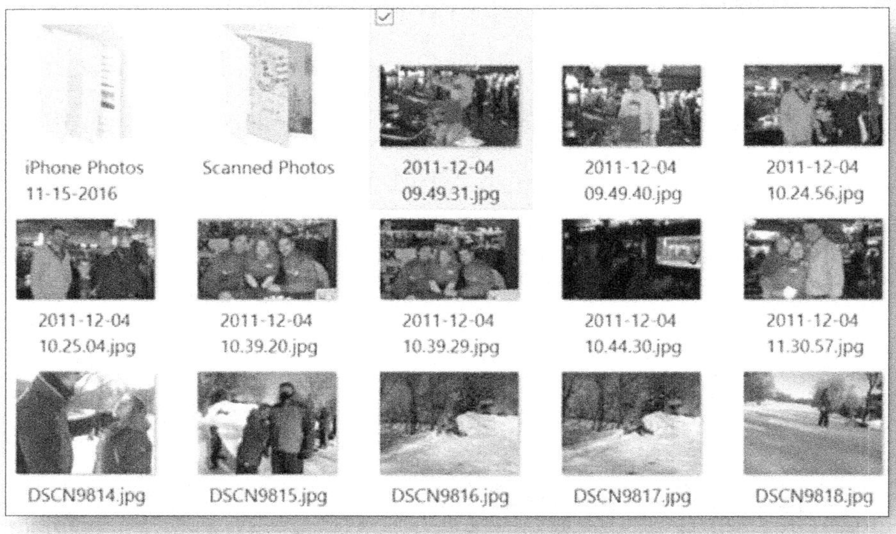

Here are two steps I can take to fix some of these issues.

Delete a few photos - The photos dated 2011-12-04 are all from when my family participated in a fundraising event at Dave & Busters. I can view these photos larger by double-clicking on one of the photos. This launches the Windows Photos app, where I can view each picture and delete the duplicates or unnecessary ones. Later in this book, I will talk more about Windows Photos. For now, it can make scrolling through and deleting photos easy. But for organizing you'll want to close the Photos app and return to File Explorer.

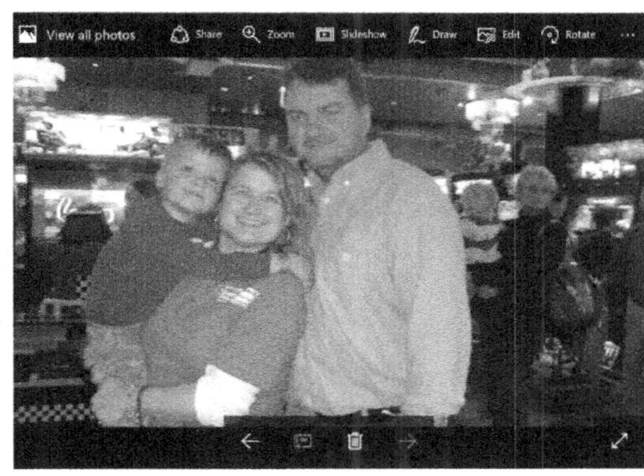

Create a folder & rename photos - Below, I made a folder for my Dave & Buster Photos. I used the YYYY-MM-DD Description format for naming the folder. I also selected those photos and right-clicked on the first photo to get a menu that allows me to rename the photos.

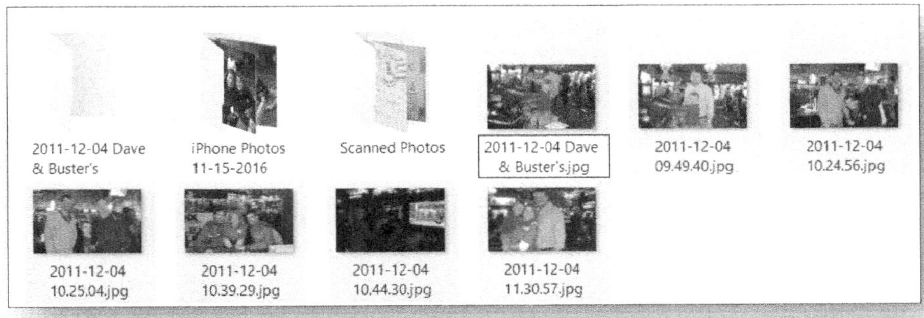

Figure 2 - File Explorer Overview

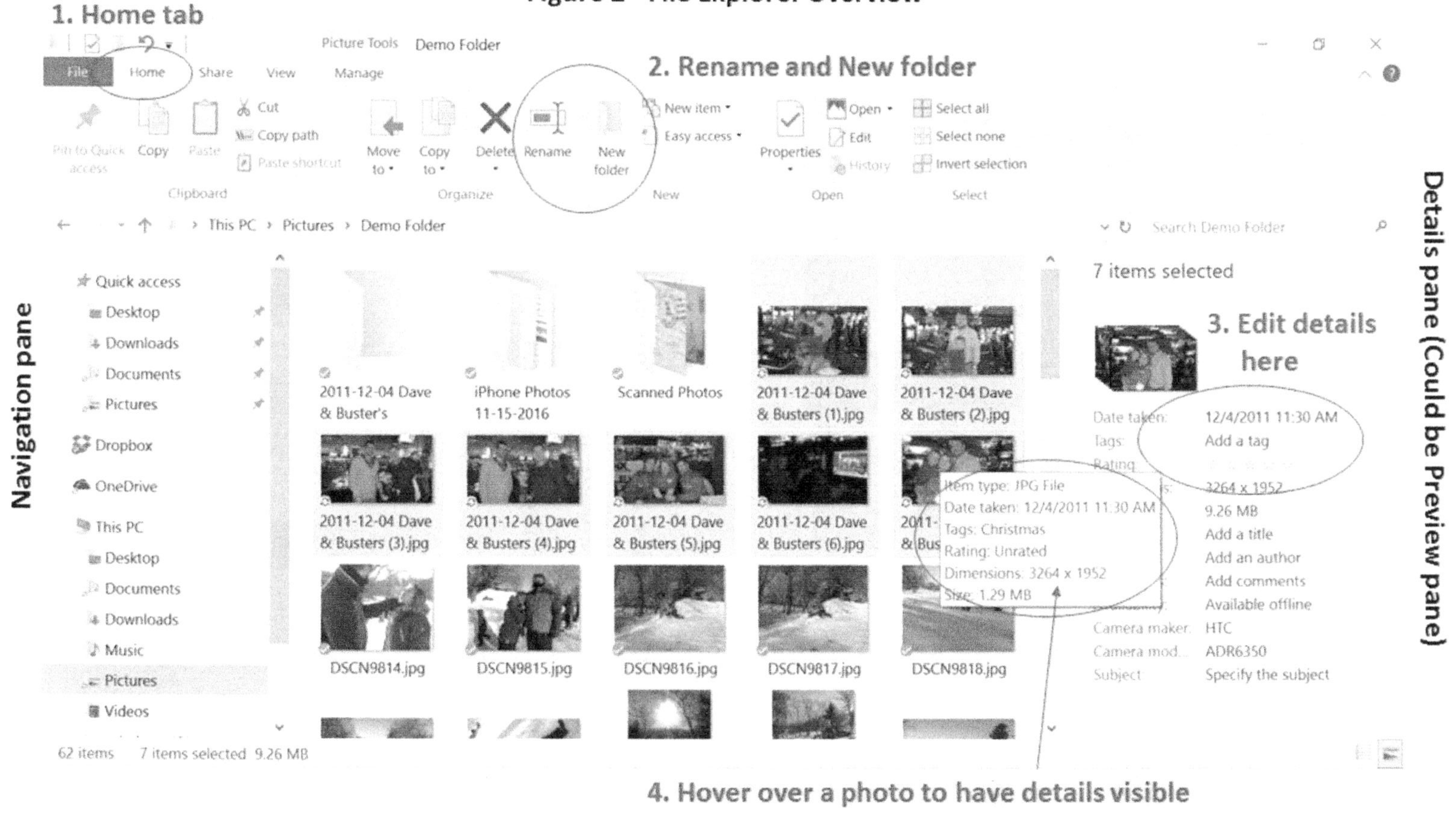

1. Home tab

2. Rename and New folder

3. Edit details here

4. Hover over a photo to have details visible

Navigation pane

Details pane (Could be Preview pane)

Picture Tools Demo Folder
File Home Share View Manage
Pin to Quick access Copy Paste Cut Copy path Paste shortcut
Clipboard
Move to Copy to Delete Rename New folder
Organize
New item Easy access
New
Properties Open Edit History
Open
Select all Select none Invert selection
Select
This PC › Pictures › Demo Folder
Search Demo Folder
Quick access
Desktop
Downloads
Documents
Pictures
Dropbox
OneDrive
This PC
Desktop
Documents
Downloads
Music
Pictures
Videos
2011-12-04 Dave & Buster's
iPhone Photos 11-15-2016
Scanned Photos
2011-12-04 Dave & Busters (1).jpg
2011-12-04 Dave & Busters (2).jpg
2011-12-04 Dave & Busters (3).jpg
2011-12-04 Dave & Busters (4).jpg
2011-12-04 Dave & Busters (5).jpg
2011-12-04 Dave & Busters (6).jpg
Item type: JPG File
Date taken: 12/4/2011 11:30 AM
Tags: Christmas
Rating: Unrated
Dimensions: 3264 x 1952
Size: 1.29 MB
DSCN9814.jpg
DSCN9815.jpg
DSCN9816.jpg
DSCN9817.jpg
DSCN9818.jpg
7 items selected
Date taken: 12/4/2011 11:30 AM
Tags: Add a tag
Rating:
3264 x 1952
9.26 MB
Add a title
Add an author
Add comments
Available offline
Camera maker: HTC
Camera mod...: ADR6350
Subject: Specify the subject
62 items 7 items selected 9.26 MB

Now let's look at **FIGURE TWO** - File Explorer Overview with the Home tab selected. Circled are the two most important functions to organize our photos: Rename and New folder. Note in this view:

1. The Home tab is selected.
2. Rename and New folder - With the Rename button, you can change the name of your folders and photos. When you select New folder, a new folder appears, and you can change the name of the folder.
3. Change details of your photo - Using the Details pane area, I can add information about these selected photos. This includes date, tags, rating and more.
4. Hover over a photo for details - Here's another way to quickly view the details of your photo. In the example here, you can see I added a tag - Christmas.

If you want to rate your photos, you may want to look at other programs to manage your photos. See Chapter 4 - Photo Organization Software Overview.

Figure 3 - File Explorer Overview

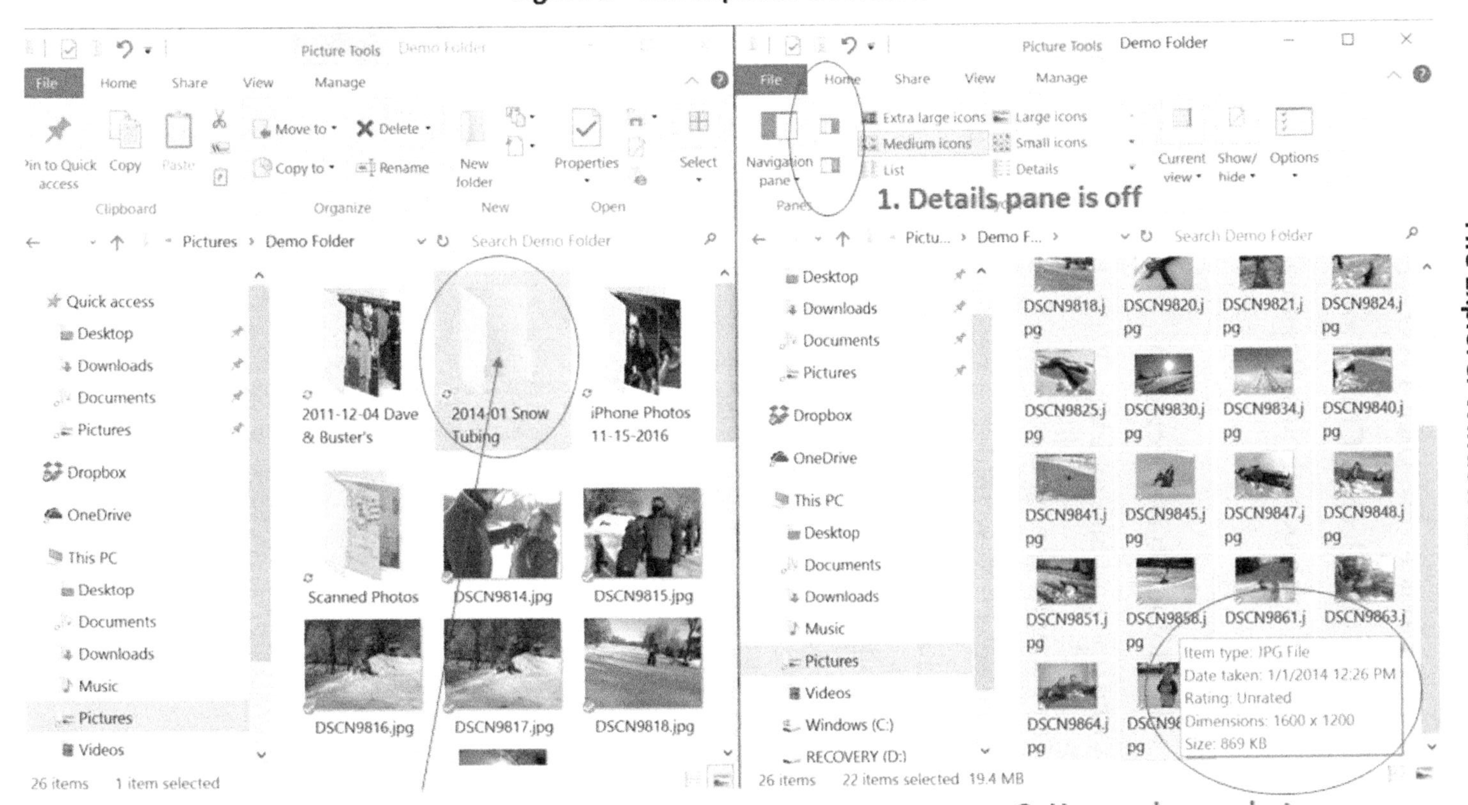

FIGURE THREE - I have added another File Explorer window. **Press the Control (ctrl) and N keys to have a new File Explorer window appear.** Or, you could also go to the File tab and click on Open new window. Having two windows open makes it a lot easier to move batches of photos around.

Not seeing exactly what you need? Check which tab is displayed on the menu (Home, View, etc.)

Note the following in this view:

1. Details pane is unselected so I have more room to see my photos - showing in Window #2 - View tab
2. By hovering over one of the snow tubing photos, I can see the information and what date it was taken so I can create a new folder with that date
3. I created a new folder in my Demo Folder labeled with the YYYY-MM-DD Description format (2014-01 Snow Tubing).

Press the Control and N keys to have a new File Explorer window appear.

Need help on having your two windows show side by side?

When you add a new window, you will want to resize their shape so the window views don't overlap significantly.

1. Hover over the edge of a window you want to resize; a little white arrow will appear. Adjust the window as needed
2. Click on the top bar of the window to move the windows around so you can view them side to side. (In the area next to the title of the window: below, Demo Folder is the title of this window.)

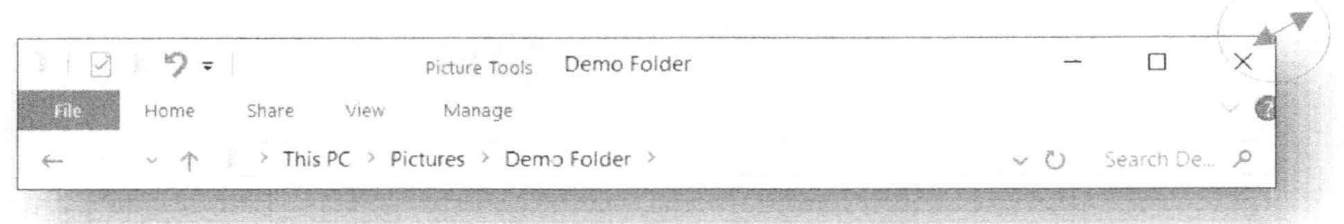

My next steps will be to work on organizing the Scanned Photos and the iPhone Photos folders. We'll come back to these examples later in this book.

Computer Tips, Tricks & Shortcuts

There are some computer tips, tricks and shortcuts that are helpful to know and can speed up your digital photo organizing. Amazingly, I have been using some of these since my college days in the 1990s. My, how far technology has come since then.

Yet these tips have stood the test of time and may even help you with other computer tasks.

PC TIP ONE - Highlighting and Selecting

When you want to do something with one file or several files, you need to select or highlight the item. Selecting one file is easy.

When we want to do the same thing with many files, we can select or highlight multiple files. You can work faster than with one file at a time and speed up the process.

Two helpful keys - Shift & Control (ctrl)

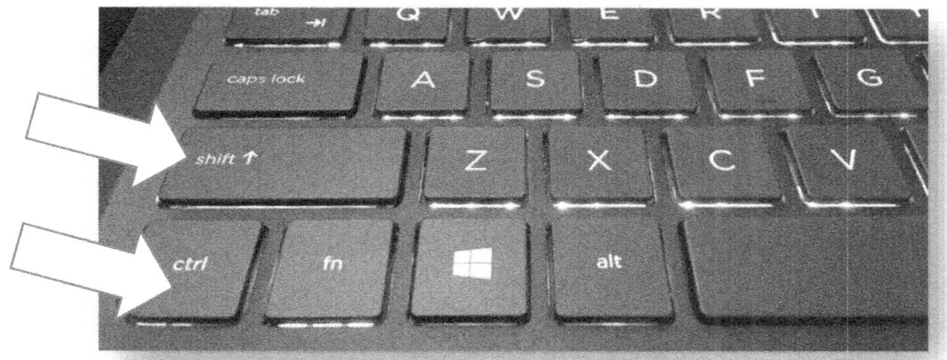

With these two keys, we have two choices in selecting groups of photos.

Select Files in a Row – Click one file, then, holding down the shift key, select the last photo in the group you want to include. All the files in between will be selected.

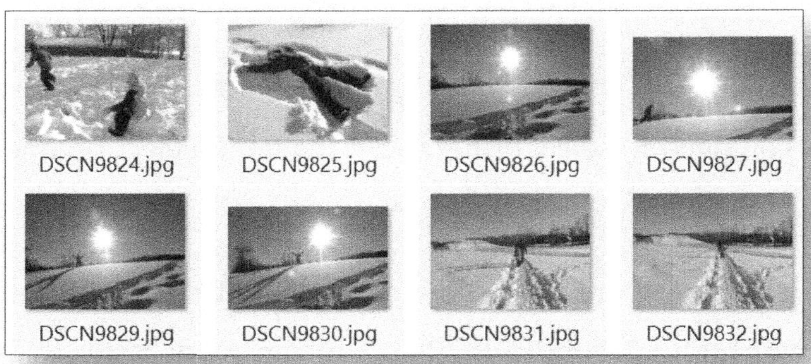

Don't want to move all of these photos? Some are pretty similar looking, right? Let's select specific photos.

Select Files One at a Time – Click one file, then, holding down the control key, click additional files you wish to highlight. You can scroll down if necessary and select more files.

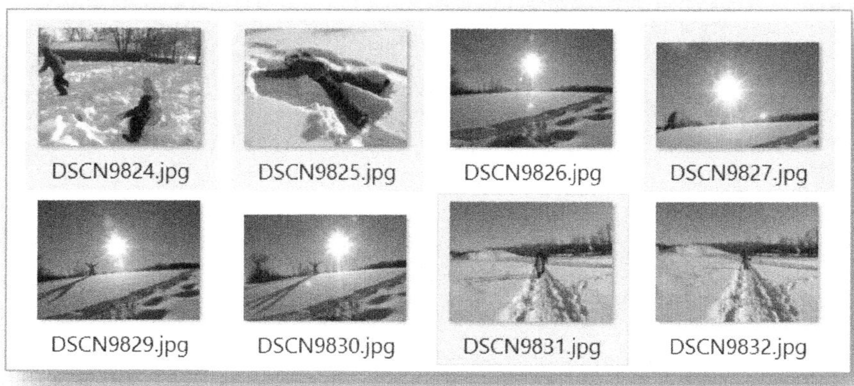

Once you have the photos selected, then you can do lots of things. Click on one of the selected photos and:

- Move the group to a new folder
- Rename the photos
- Delete them

So, what else can you do with files once you have them selected? A great lead-in to our next topic . . . the left-click and right-click function of your mouse!

PC TIP TWO – Left-Click/Right-Click

Your computer's mouse should be your best friend. A touchpad works, but a mouse provides more control and precision. If you are using a laptop, I recommend getting a mouse if you don't have one. (A wireless mouse costs just $10 to $20 for an inexpensive one; and they come in fun colors now.)

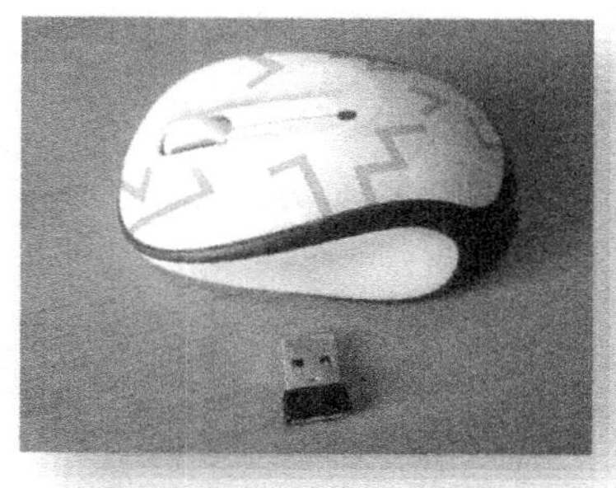

In my client work, I meet people who don't understand left-clicking and right-clicking. In virtually every program, the left-click and right-click function very similarly.

Left-click – Selects or highlights something (text, photos, files, etc.)

Double left-click – Opens a file or program

Right-click – Gives you a menu of what you can do with the item or area you selected with a left-click. See below for the menu that appears when you right-click a photo.

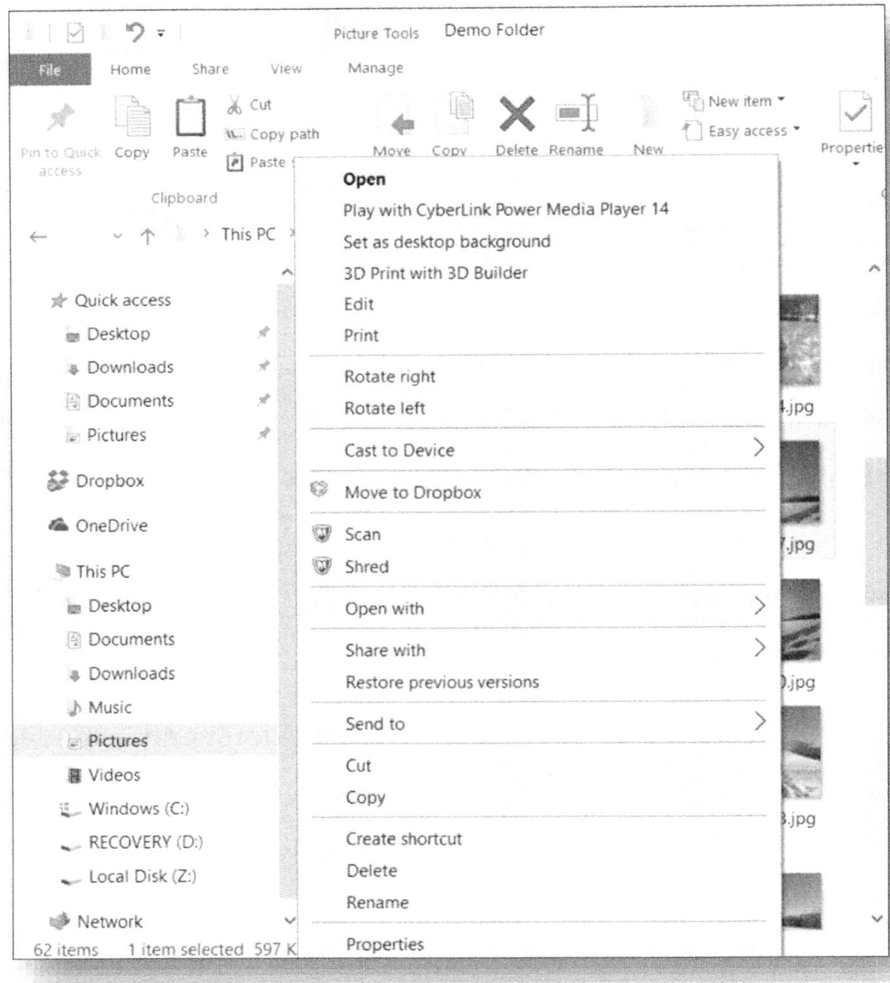

Look at all the options available to us. Mostly we care about these tasks:

- Rotate left or right
- Open with – To open with a certain program
- Rename – Make a simpler name for your photos
- Properties – Gives great information about the photo. We saw this in the Details Pane previously. There a few tabs, and I selected the Details tab to show you here. See all the digital information that a photo can contain?
    - Title
    - Rating
    - Tags
    - Comments
    - Date taken
    - Image details

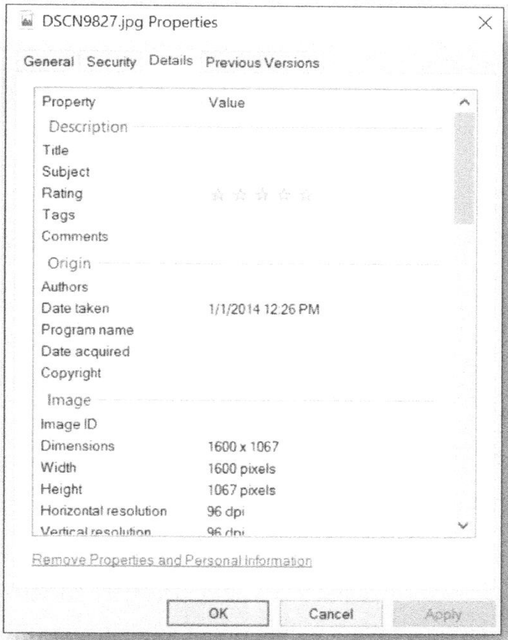

With this tab, you can edit the fields here to add more information about your photo or correct the date it was taken.

Now, let's get back to right-clicking. There is another area that is helpful to right-click within. That is in the open space area of your File Explorer window. In the example below, I right-clicked in the open area on the bottom to have the menu appear.

Here you can see our menu options include some important items.

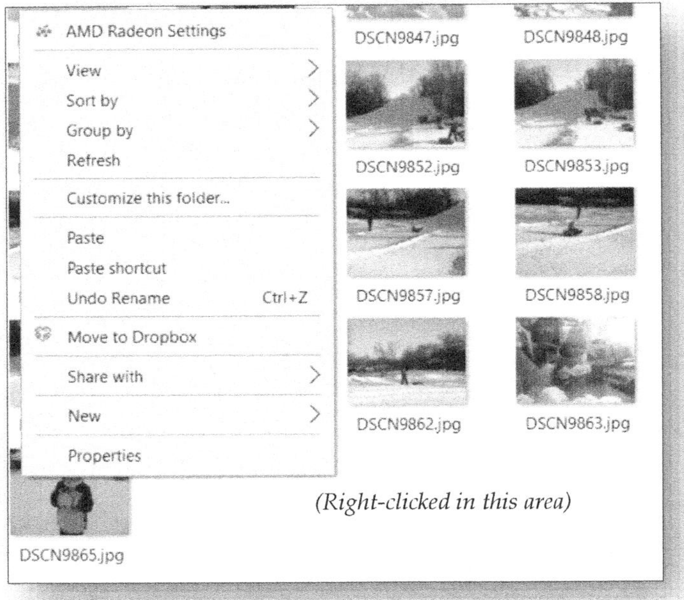

- Paste - I had previously copied a file and could click Paste for it to be put in this folder. (Cut and Copy are not an option because I haven't selected a file. I only right-clicked in the empty area of the folder.)
- New - Here you can click on the arrow and get more options (in the example on the next page, the menu popped

out to the left). The most important option is the New Folder. You can ignore everything else for our purposes.

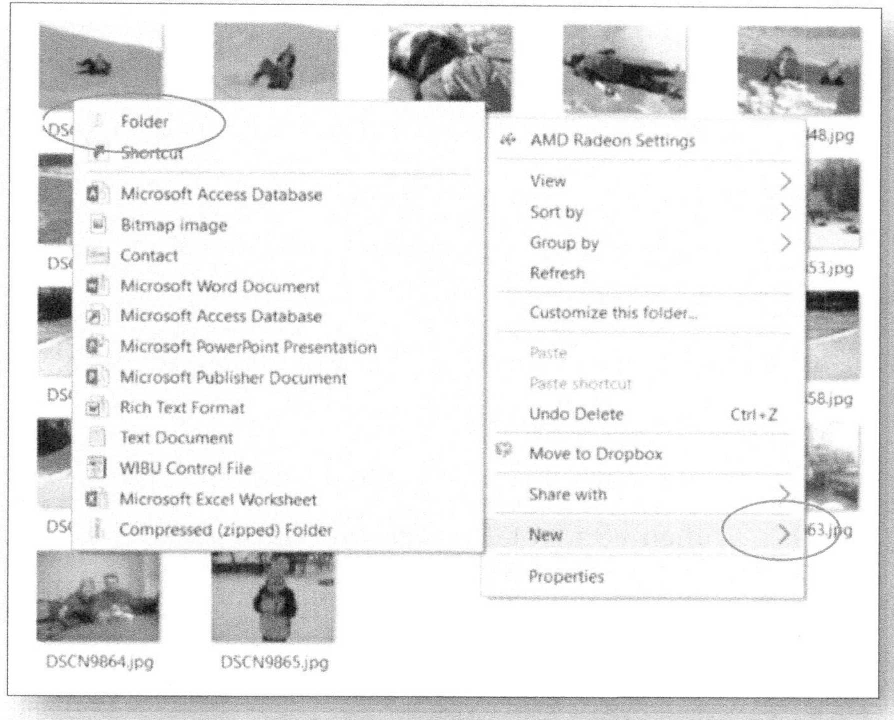

Creating folders easily is important to organizing photos. We'll be showing two other ways in this chapter. We have found that often there are many ways to do the same task on a computer. Find the method that works for you, and stick with it!

PC TIP THREE – Some Quick Keys to Know

Instead of using menus, you can use quick keys to do a task. Once you have selected something, you can let go of your mouse and go to your keyboard to press the following keys:

- Control (ctrl) + N = Creates a new folder or a new window
- Control (ctrl) + A = Select all (click on one photo and then Control + A)
- Control (ctrl) + Z = Undo (works in many programs to undo your last action)
    - Great for when you select a bunch of photos and then accidentally click on copy. (Happens all the time to our clients.) All of sudden, you have duplicate digital pictures. Undo it quick!
- Control (crtl) + C = Copy
- Control (crtl) + X = Cut
- Control (crtl) + V = Paste

While I love the quick keys for copy, cut and paste, I don't recommend using them to move files from one folder to another. If you accidentally cut photos from one folder and somehow miss pasting them to another, you can lose photos. I much prefer moving folders by dragging them from one folder to another.

PC TIP FOUR - Dragging Folders or Files

In the example below, I clicked on the 100NC151 folder (my camera card of photos) and dragged it to the Pictures folder. You can see the little photo of my folder being moved with a note that says Copy to Pictures.

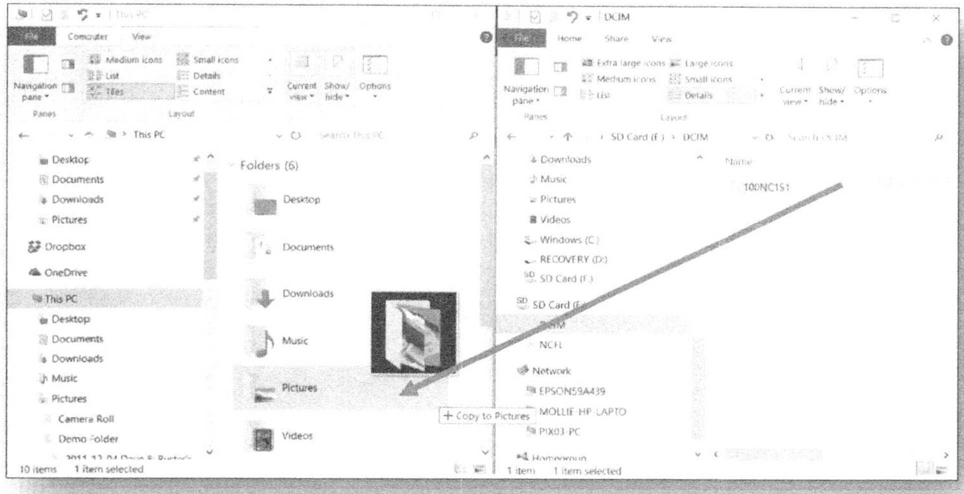

Dragging files or folders from an external source (camera card, jump drive, etc.) - your files are being COPIED to your computer. The photos are still stored on that external source.

Dragging files or folders within your computer (file folder to file folder) - your files are being MOVED to the new location on your computer from the old location. This means they are no longer located in that original folder.

Wrapping Up Computer Skills

We have covered a lot of material about using Windows File Explorer. As you probably can see, remembering how to do these tips, tricks and shortcuts will take practice.

If you organize your photos monthly, mastering these skills will be much easier. Consistently organizing and saving your photos will produce a great family photo collection.

CHAPTER THREE – BRING IT ALL TOGETHER

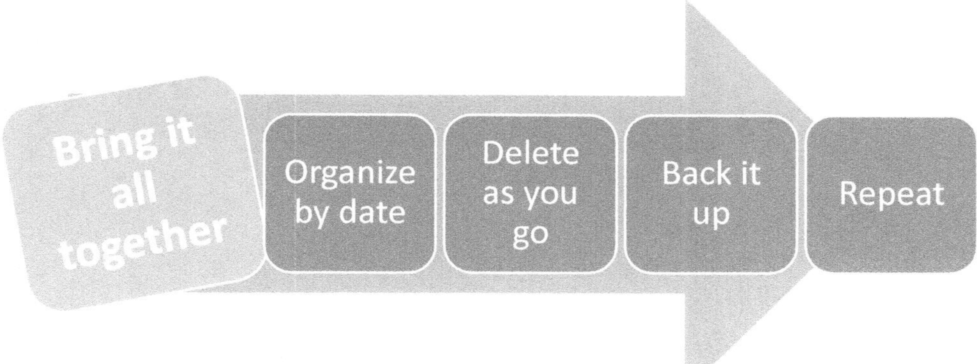

Want to tackle and conquer your digital photo mess once and for all? It's time to gather all your photos to one place!

The concept of "bringing it all together" has two meanings for our purposes. First, you'll want to bring anything that has a digital photo on it to one place. Second, we will move all the photos to one location on your computer in the "Pictures" folder.

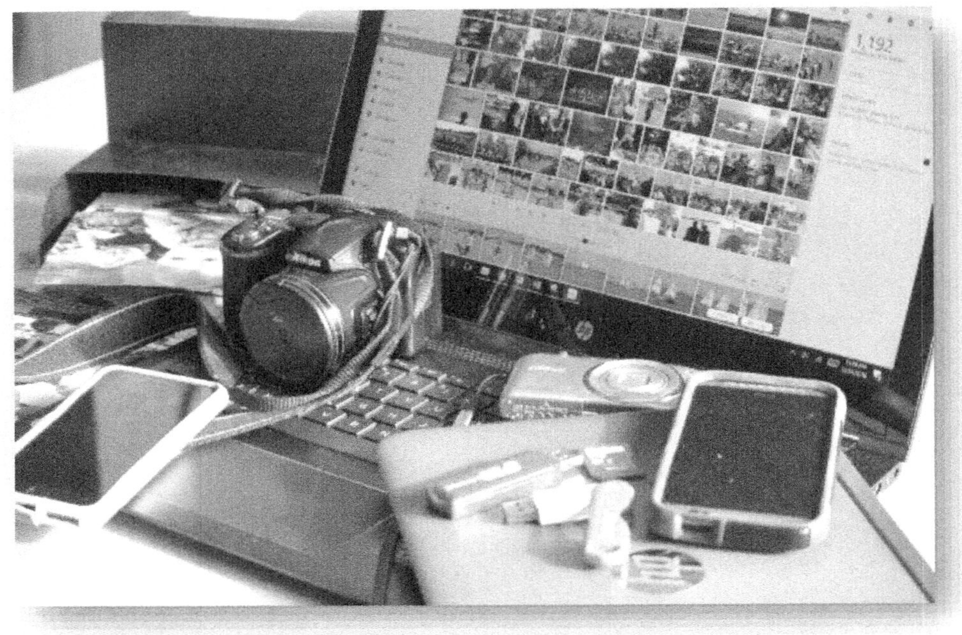

Gathering All Your Devices Together

Bring It All Together Meaning #1 – Most people have digital photos in more than three locations. Once we left the 1990s and entered the 2000s, digital photography grew rapidly. So did the options for how we could save our digital photos. If you can think of several places where you have stored digital photos, then it is time to fix the situation.

There are many places where digital photos can be found. Let's start gathering your photos to store in one location. In some cases, my clients put these items in a basket until they are ready to get to work on their computer.

Here's a list of potential places your digital photos may be residing. It's amazing how, with each bullet point, you could have multiple copies of digital photos. The last two bullet points represent places where you may have photos located online.

- Cameras/camera cards
- CDs/DVDs
- Jump Drives/external hard drives
- Older computers
- Smartphones/text messages
- iPads/tablets
- Shutterfly, Walgreens & more
- Email/social media

Bringing Your Photos to Your Computer

Bring It All Together Meaning #2 – Now that we have devices ready to connect to our computer, we will start the true work of gathering all your photos to one place. This one place is the Pictures folder on your computer. Sounds like it should be easy. However, each device may have its own instructions to save photos. Next, we'll go over how to connect each of these devices to your computer.

Keep in mind that most of the devices that connect to your computer will appear as another "drive." Your computer is treating your device as a hard drive with files stored within it. This means your device or devices will appear in the File Explorer Navigation pane.

Generally, CDs/DVDs will show up as your D: drive. Other devices will be assigned to the drive based on what USB port was used to connect to the computer.

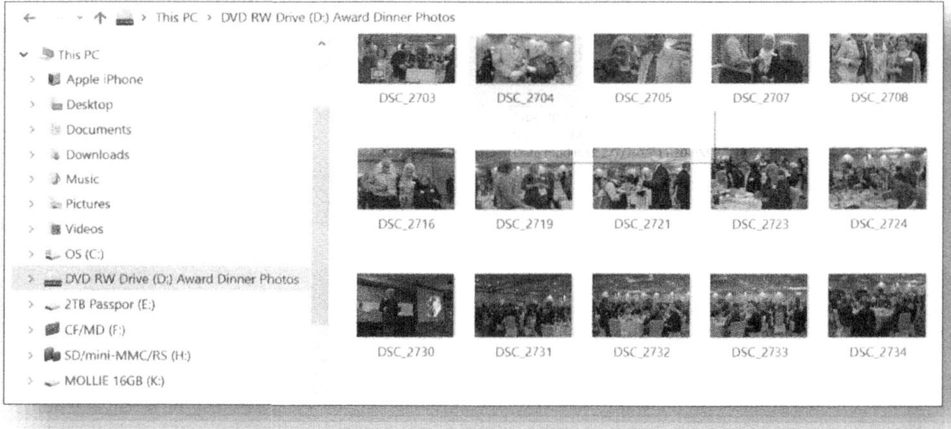

In the screenshot above, you can see I have several drive letters appearing under "This PC." My iPhone is also listed. That's a lot of drives! For organizing purposes, you may wish to connect one device at a time.

Here are the devices I have connected to my computer:

- Apple iPhone – My iPhone
- DVD RW Drive (D:) – A DVD of photos from a dinner
- 2TB Passpor (E:) – My 2 TB external hard drive
- CF/MD (F:) – An old Compact Flash camera card
- SD/mini-MMC/RS (H:) – My current Nikon camera card
- MOLLIE 16GB (K:) – My Lexar jump drive

When copying photos over to your computer, the easiest way is to create two File Explorer windows. Then drag folders over to your Pictures folder. See below; I have my SD Card folder (named 100NC151) in the right window. I dragged it over to my Pictures folder in the left window. It's working because I see the prompt that says "Copy to Pictures."

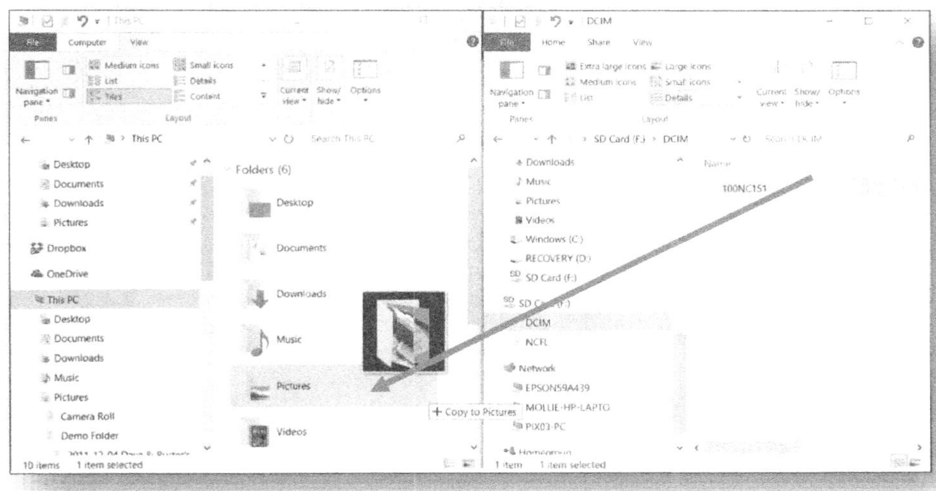

Because we covered using two window views in the previous chapter, we won't spend time on screen shots. We will focus on features and characteristics of the different devices.

Below you can see I have copied a variety of device folders into my demo folder. I did rename the 100NC151 folder to something that made sense to me – the Nikon SD Camera Card folder.

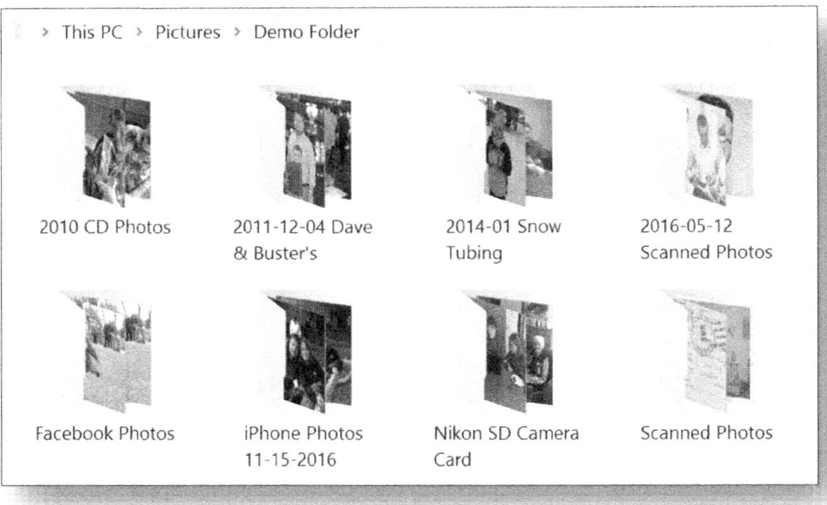

Each time you finish working on your Pictures folder, you should back it up to an external hard drive. We'll cover options for this in Chapter Five.

So now, let's cover the different devices you'll be connecting to your computer.

Camera Cards

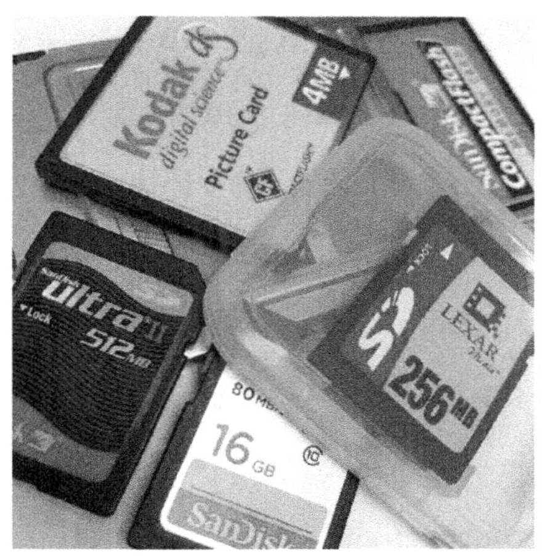

Since digital cameras were introduced, camera cards have changed shapes and sizes.

Some of our clients have always filled a new camera card and then bought a new one when needed. We have seen some clients with lots of cards to copy. These cards are small, fragile and easily lost. Your photos should never be stored on camera cards.

Copy the camera cards to your Pictures folder and then set aside the camera cards with a note they are copied.

If you know the specific date range you can rename it. In the screenshot, I added 2010 Misc to the folder name.

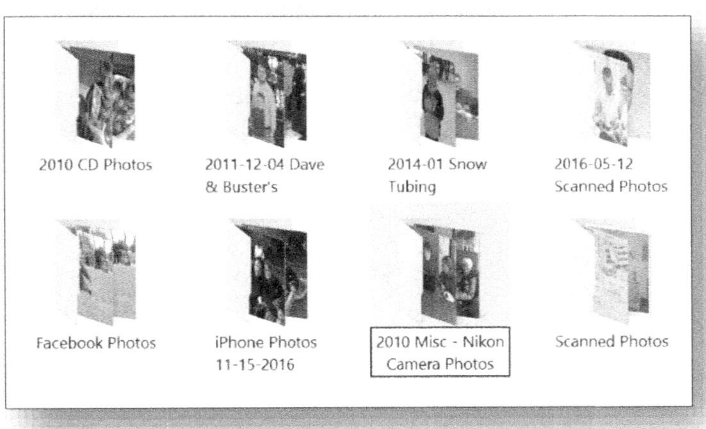

Cameras

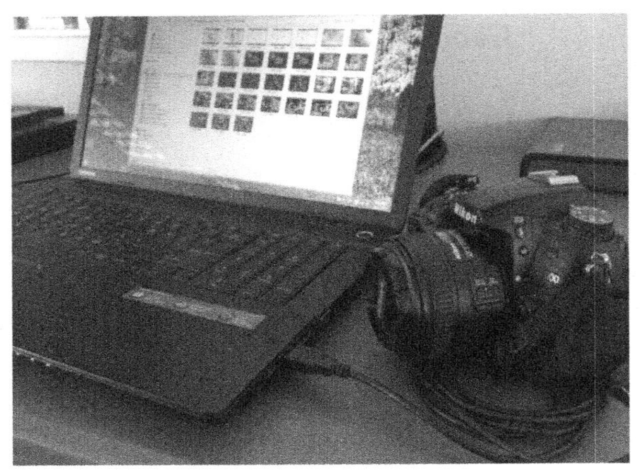

Generally, people do not store photos on their cameras. However, occasionally some of the photos end up on the camera's internal storage. To get these pictures off your camera, the photos need to be transferred to the Camera Card. Consult your camera manual if you have this situation. Another option is to connect your camera to your computer using a USB Cable.

CDs & DVDs

In the 2000s, CDs and DVDs provided consumers a safe, understandable way to save their photos. Today, most new laptop computers do not even come with a DVD drive. Old CDs and DVDs can fail. One of our clients had over 300 CDs dated from 2004 to 2009. Over 50 CDs were unreadable and the photos were lost. Copy the photos off your CDs and DVDs and into your computer's Pictures folder.

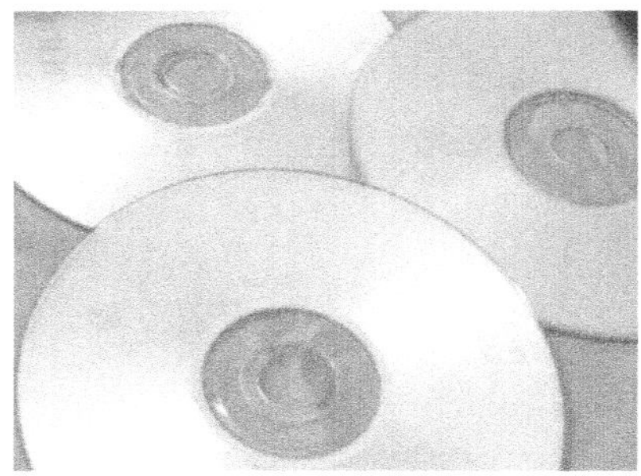

Jump Drives

Jump drives are called USB flash drives, thumb drives, memory sticks, etc. They are available in an unlimited sizes, shapes and colors. Easily lost or misplaced, these drives should only be used to transport or share photos. If you have photos stored on jump drives, move them to your Pictures folder in a folder.

External Hard Drives

We work with two types of external hard drives depending upon the situation. Some of our clients have external drives, and some have never seen one before.

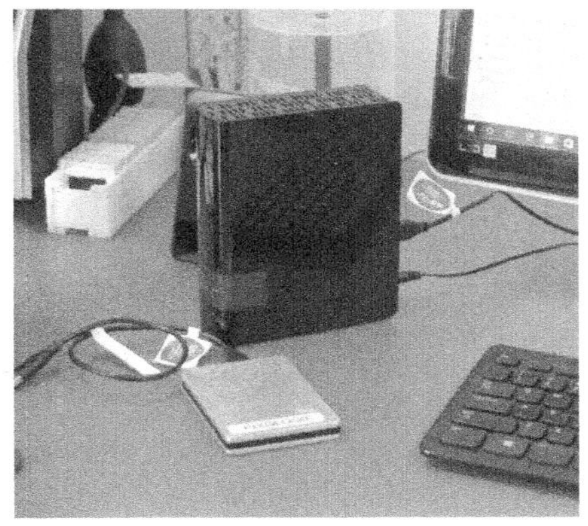

See two types of external drives here. The small, flat drive is portable. The tall box is a desktop version. Notice it has a power supply. Both drives have a USB 3.0 label – the newest technology for these drives.

You can find several types of external hard drives at any office supply or electronics store. Each year the size of external hard drives goes up and the price comes down. If you don't have an external hard drive, you should buy at least one to function as your backup.

USB 3.0 refers to the USB cable connecting speed. It can be distinguished by the blue coloring located within the connectors. Why is it important? USB 3.0 helps your files copy to your external hard drive up to 10 times faster.

Desktop, High Capacity Drives

These type of drives have two cords, one for power and one for the USB cable. If the device is not plugged in, your computer will not be able to open any of the files on it.

A piece of advice if you own this type of drive . . . Do not keep it powered on all the time, day-in and day-out, if you are using it as a backup system. Running these type of drives for an extended period of time can wear out the power supply and other mechanical parts. This results in poor performance. Files take a very long time to load and, eventually, the drive can fail. These drives are not meant to travel and should remain at home in the same location.

Our clients use external hard drives in different ways:

- To save space on their computers

- As the place where they have backed up their files from other computers. but never return to clean up the files
- To transport photos to other family members or locations

In each of these situations, there are risks to storing photos on an external hard drive. These drives can fail, be dropped or be lost. Just like with any other storage device, these accumulate easily. You can lose track of what you have saved and where you have saved it.

Our recommendation: Use external hard drives for routinely backing up the photos on your computer, not as a working device.

We have met people who do store the majority of their photos on an external hard drive. They are typically professionals who have large photo collections. We have met photographers and artists who have hundreds of thousands of photos.

If you are unable to keep your photo collection on your computer, then be sure to back up that drive to two separate places.

Some people store photos on an external hard drive because they don't know how to best save their photos. If this is your situation, you need to copy those photos to your computer. Just to review how to do this:

1. Connect your USB cord from the drive to your computer and open your File Explorer. Your external hard drive will appear in the left pane with a different drive letter from your C: Drive.
2. Copy the photos or folders of photos to your Pictures folder.

In the example below, my external hard drive appears as the E: drive, and when I select it, I can see a few folders. I am going to copy the 2016-05 Scanned Photos folder by dragging it over to

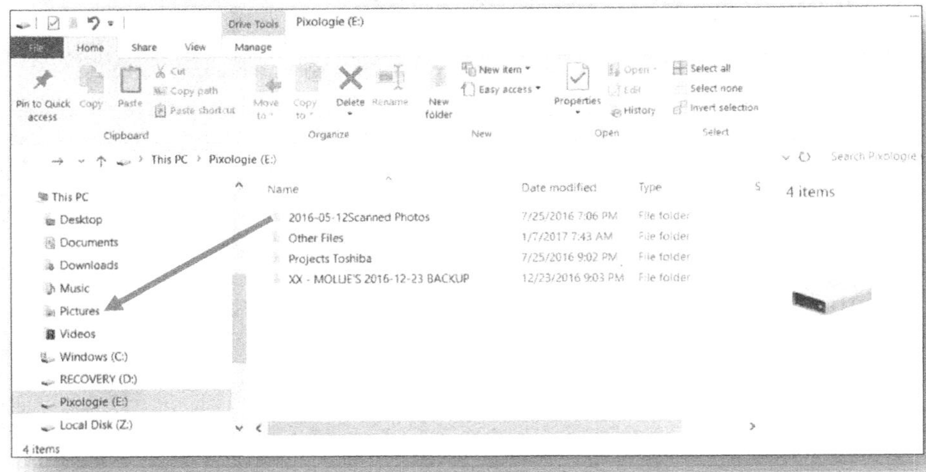

the Pictures folder. When I have completed copying folders over to my computer, I like to put an XX in front of the folder I copied. Then I'll remember I already copied that folder. You can see this in the figure below. (Need to remember how to rename a folder or file? Right-click on the folder or file for a menu of options, or click on the Rename button in the Home tab.) Here's my renamed folders:

Name	Date modified	Type
Other Files	1/7/2017 7:43 AM	File folder
Projects Toshiba	7/25/2016 9:02 PM	File folder
XX - 2016-05-12Scanned Photos	7/25/2016 7:06 PM	File folder
XX - MOLLIE'S 2016-12-23 BACKUP	12/23/2016 9:03 PM	File folder

I also need reminders that I have copied files from devices. See below for my Post-its! You could add notes about what is on each device if that would be useful for you.

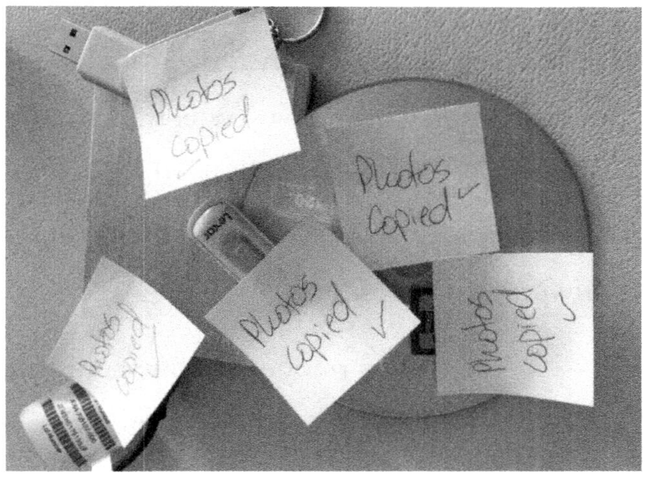

Smartphones

Consumers are using their smartphones as their sole camera. Some smartphones offer photo backup such as iCloud (iPhone) or Google Photos (Android). This can provide temporary security of having your photos backed up. However, we do not recommend it for a long-term solution. iCloud has limited free storage space, and Google Photos has some user permissions you may not wish to grant Google.

There are other types of programs that will automatically copy photos from your phone to a folder. Dropbox and OneDrive are examples. While this is a quick solution to saving photos to your computer, often it leads to confusion and bad habits. I recommend turning off the automatic transfer. If you have this situation, see Appendix A for more information about Dropbox and/or OneDrive.

We recommend manually transferring pictures from your phone to your computer. This gives you better control over how your photos are saved. ***Important note: Before plugging your phone into your computer, delete all the photos from your phone you know you don't need to save.***

iPhone – Connect your phone to your computer with its USB cord. Wait for the device to appear in your Navigation pane.

Sometimes, your phone may not appear on your first try. Unplug your phone and try again if this happens. Once connected, your phone may ask if you would like to give the computer access to your phone. You'll want to allow access.

Photos will be in the DCIM folder and contain one or a series of folders. You can copy the folders or the individual photos to your Pictures folder.

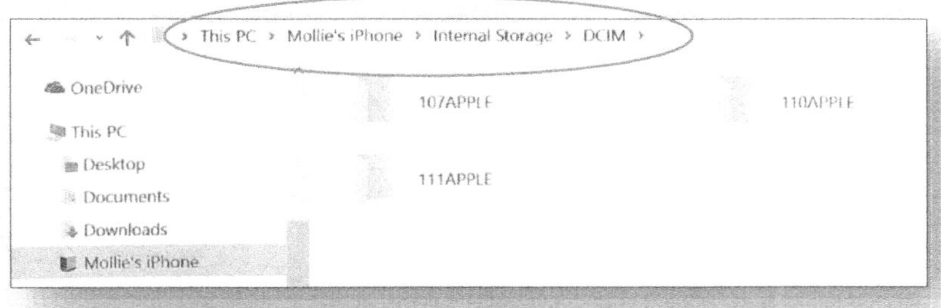

Here's a screenshot of dragging the photos from the 110APPLE folder and to a new folder I created in the Pictures folder. (Refer to page 34 if necessary.)

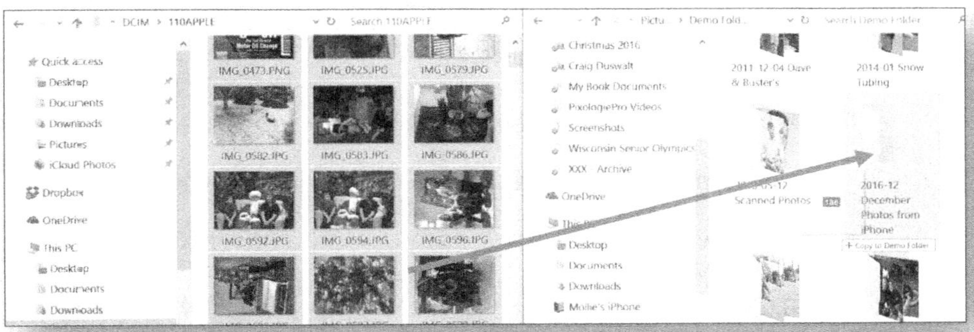

Android Phone – Photos on an Android phone can be found in two places sometimes: on your phone's internal storage or on a memory card located within your phone. Like the iPhone example, connect your Android phone to your computer with its USB cable. Once you have done that, your phone will appear in your File Explorer as a separate drive.

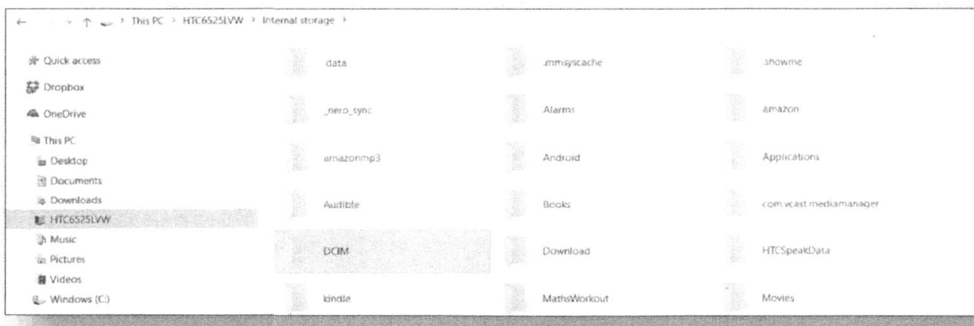

You'll need to find the folder where your pictures are stored and then copy them to a folder in your Pictures folder. See above; my HTC phone has a DCIM folder also.

To refresh your memory, there's a couple of ways to do this:

1. Drag the entire folder over to your Pictures folder. Rename the folder with a date (could be the date of the photos contained or the date of your folder transfer)
    - 2016-10 October Photos from Samsung
    - 2016-10 Samsung Phone Photos to be organized

2. Or. . . Select the individual picture files you wish to copy to your computer's Pictures folder

Once you are done transferring the photos over to your computer, you can unplug your phone.

If you are diligent about backing up your Pictures folder, then you can delete the photos from your phone. Sometimes our clients like to keep their pictures on their phone. That is fine, if you have space on your phone. You also need to have a good system of knowing which photos you have already saved and which you haven't.

Text Messages

Often I'll receive a photo in a text message which I want to keep. If you use a smartphone, chances are you have texts with photos.

If you want to save these pictures, save them to your smartphone from the text message. Simply click on the photo in the text message and select the save option. The photo can be found in your Photos app on your phone.

iPads and Tablets

Do you take photos with an iPad or tablet? I have seen people do this and these function in much the same way as a smartphone. You'll connect you tablet to your computer and, again, the device will show up as a drive in your File Explorer.

Shutterfly, Walgreens & More

For two decades, people have been able to upload photos and order prints from online providers. In some instances, I have had clients tell me that this is where their photos are stored and saved.

There are problems with relying on online print providers as the home of your photos. Can you think of some instances where this could be a problem? Consider these situations:

- In July of 2015, Costco, Sam's Club, CVS Pharmacy, Rite Aid and many other retailers shut down their photo sites. This was due to potential customer information being stolen. Several weeks went by when customers had no access to their photo files. (Reuters, July 20, 2015)
- In October 2016, a massive online attack shut down access to many popular websites including Twitter, Paypal, Amazon and more. In addition, many homes were unable to connect to the internet for nearly a day. (USA Today, October 2016)

I am skeptical of any internet service or website being secure. Consider all the news about hacked emails, websites and internet viruses that have appeared just in the last year.

Take all of internet security issues out of the equation, and I am still skeptical. Consider the power needed to run your computer and devices to connect to the internet. We are one extended power outage away from losing access to our photos that are stored online.

In addition, the effort to download photos from these sites can be intimidating.

- Some sites only allow you to download one photo at a time
- Downloaded photos may be of a lower quality than you originally uploaded
- Photos may have none of the digital data from their original upload (e.g., date taken, original file name from camera)

Lastly, these businesses are being bought, closed down or put up for sale at a dizzying rate. You can never be sure the next owner will maintain the site the way you are used to, or even if they will maintain it at all.

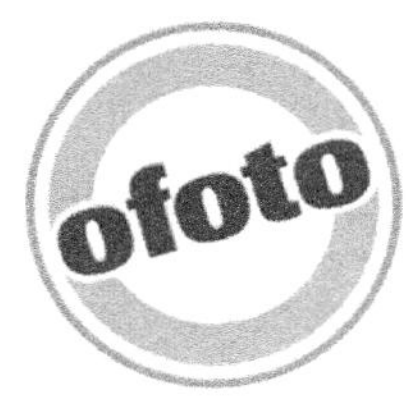

Do you remember Ofoto? This company was acquired by Kodak in 2001. By 2008, Kodak EasyShare Gallery had over 60 million users. Four short years later, Kodak went into bankruptcy and Shutterfly took over Kodak's photo processing business. I was an Ofoto user, but I have no clue when and where my photos are today. Fortunately, I did pay nearly $100 to receive my photos on a CD in the mid 2000s and saved them to my computer. Shutterfly itself has been the focus of offers from a variety of sources both in 2015 and 2016.

For clients who rely on Shutterfly for their photo storage, we recommend they keep a full copy of those files located within their home.

So do you have photos located with an online print provider? If these are your only copies, then we recommend you download them to your computer and save them in your Pictures folder.

Often when you download photos you can find them in your Downloads folder. Move them to your Pictures folder.

Email

When someone emails you a photo you wish to keep, download it. Then move it to the appropriate folder in your Pictures folder. When someone emails you a link to share photos they have taken, go to that link and download the desired photos. Sometimes, the download will be a zipped file of photos. You can double click the zipped file and extract the photos. Again, move them to your Pictures folder.

Social Media - Facebook

Facebook has revolutionized how we share photos with our families and friends since it launched over 10 years ago. I love Facebook and have used it since 2009. Many times, this is how I share photos. My family and friends can download photos from events we have attended together. And, vice versa, I have downloaded the shared photos from friends and family.

A few things to consider with Facebook photos:

- At this time, Facebook does not keep any of the digital information about the photo (original date taken, people you've tagged, etc.) In addition, you may be downloading a lower quality photo than originally uploaded.
- Anyone with access to your timeline can download your photos. You must check your privacy settings because, in some cases, these people may not even be a Facebook friend.

- You can download single images easily. But if want to download more than one at a time, you need to use a third-party software program.

So do you have photos stored on Facebook that you want to have in your permanent collection? Then it is time to download the photos to your Pictures folder on your computer.

When you select the Photos tab on your Facebook profile page, you should see three categories of photos to choose from.

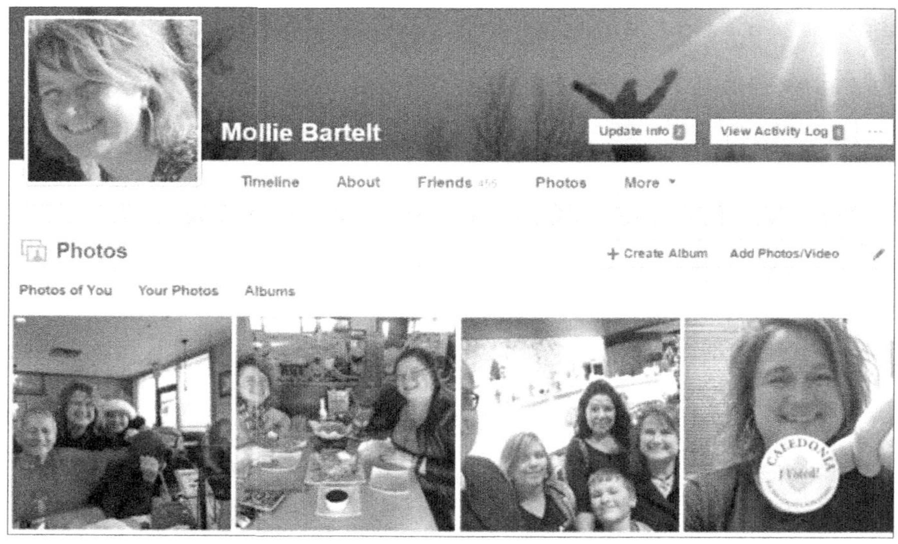

Photos of You – Includes your photos as well as photos you have been tagged in.

Your Photos – Includes all photos you have uploaded.

Albums - Includes:

- Videos
- Mobile Uploads - Photos from your phone
- Timeline Photos - Anything you have posted to your timeline
- Any other album you have created. For instance, I created a Christmas Eve Breakfast album and shared it with my family. They were able to download the photos they wanted.

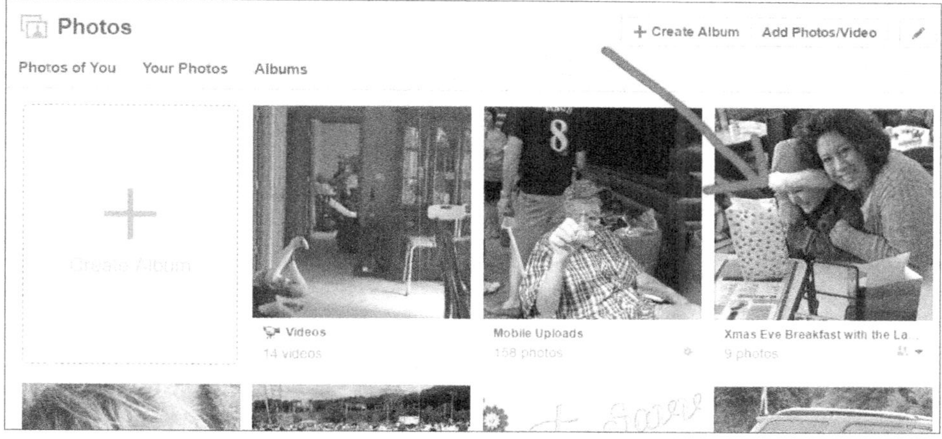

How to download:

1. Go to the picture you want to download, and click on it to view it

2. In the photo below, you can see the menu that appears when you right-click on the photo
3. Select "Save Image As," and then you can designate where you want to save the photo
4. Give it a name that is meaningful. Perhaps the date and subject like 2010-10-31 Alex Soccer (I found the date under my name.)

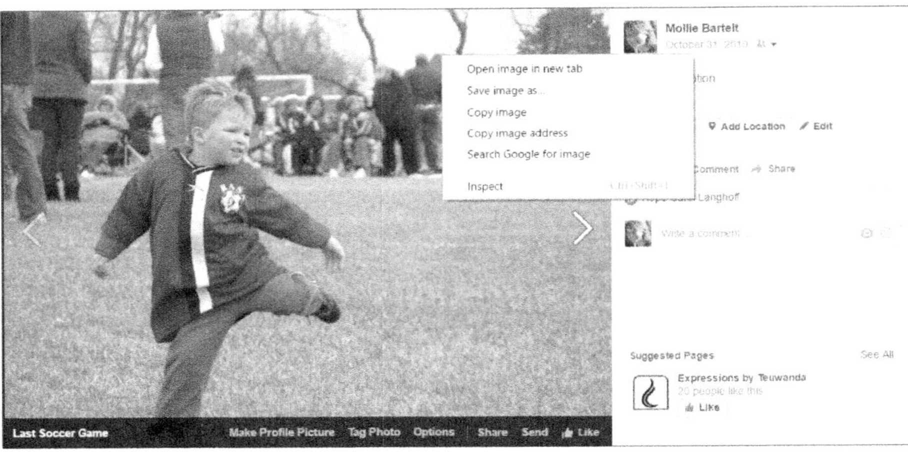

You are also able to download Facebook photos by clicking on the Options tab in the black bar. However, this results in an automatic download to your "Downloads" folder with a useless numerical name.

Compare the two photo files on the next page, where I have saved them both to a Facebook Photos folder in my Pictures folder. Note that I have named the left one with the date first, easily found in the post from Facebook when I downloaded it. You can see in the right photo the long name Facebook gave the picture using the Option-Download method, and I had to move it to this folder from my Downloads folder.

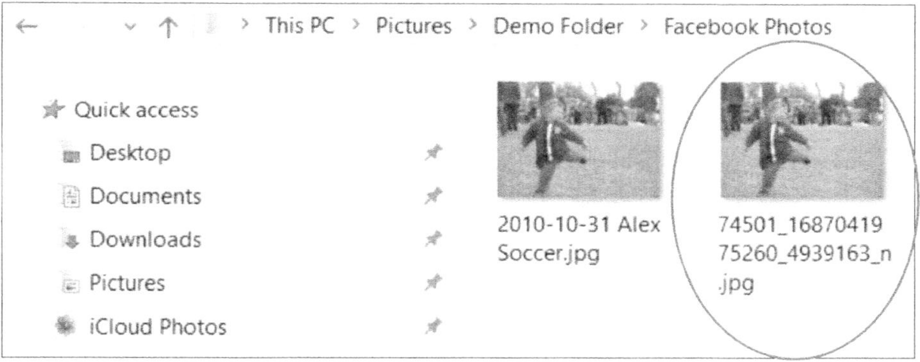

There are so many other social media sites where you can have photos stored or photos you want to keep. From Twitter, Instagram and others, you will find similar issues with downloading photos. Back in 2014, USA Today reporter Rob Pegoraro wrote, "On the Internet, what goes up does not always come down as easily." It's still true today.

Each month, we recommend reviewing all your social media sites. Download and save the photos that you want. I know what is like to search through Facebook posts trying to find a missing photo. It's a pain, especially if the photo is years old.

Wrapping This Up

We have finally covered the major topics of where your photos might be stored. We've also described how you can move them to one single place on your computer - in your Pictures folder.

Using all of these tips, here's what my Demo Folder looks like now:

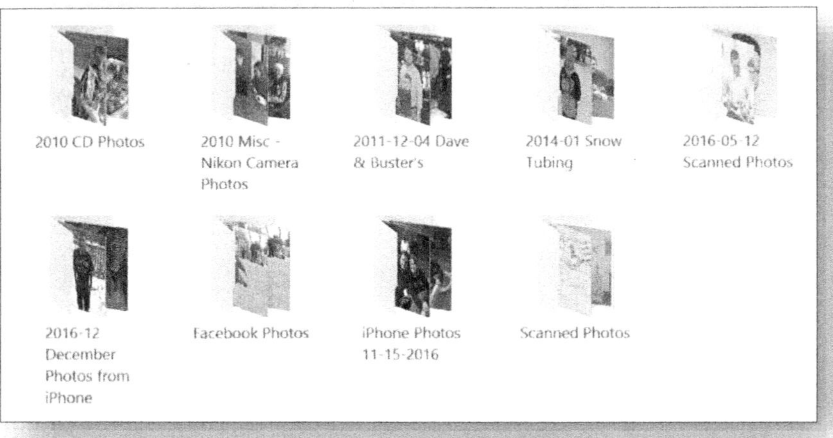

We've brought all these photos to one place; now we can sort them chronologically.

CHAPTER FOUR – ORGANIZE BY DATE

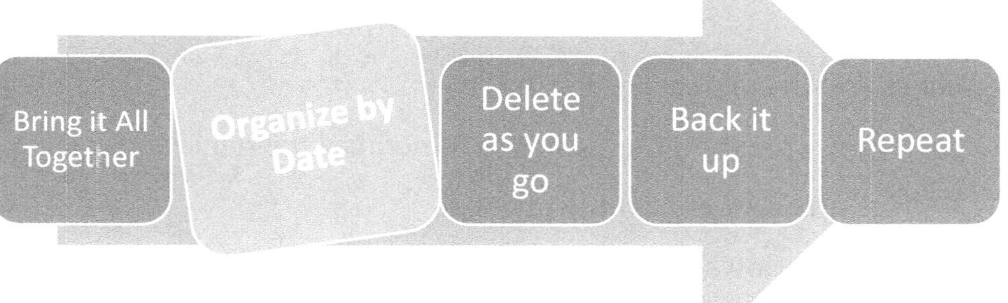

Now that we have all of our photos in the Pictures folder, we can start organizing photos so you can find the pictures you need when you want them. I'll be explaining the process for organizing photos using Windows File Explorer first. Then, I will provide examples of photo organization software we recommend to clients who want more than File Explorer.

Naming System for Your Folders – YYYY-MM-DD

Now that you know a little bit about File Explorer, let's talk further about how we name our folders. You can name your folders in different ways like:

- Chronologically
- By family member
- By other categories (work, vacation, etc.)

Our recommendation is to name folders by the date of the pictures contained within the folder. We use the system:

YYYY-MM-DD Description

There are several reasons for this:

- More often, it is easier to remember the general date of an event to find the photo
- Windows sorts the folders in numerical order. You can easily see which photos are in each folder
- It's easier to find pictures by year for family photo projects like albums and calendars
- You don't have to think hard when saving your photos on a monthly basis about where they go

Examples of using this formula include:

- 2016-10 October Photos
- 2016-10 Wisconsin Dells Trip

- 2016-10-31 Halloween Photos

Whatever your system is in naming your folders, you'll want to be consistent with it.

Types of Digital Photo Files

It may be helpful to know what the different digital photo file formats are as you organize your pictures.

JPGs - Most digital cameras and phones save pictures as JPGs. This format does involve some file compression. For most consumers, JPGs are the typical file format used. Be aware: the typical file size is 1 to 8 MB per photo. Any smaller, and you might find some pixilation when you print the photo.

TIFFs - Highest-quality, uncompressed photos. Some cameras can be set to take TIFF photos; however, the files are huge. This type of digital format is used by professionals who heavily edit, archive and more with the photos.

PNGs - If you take screenshots or download photos from the web, the digital files might be PNG.

RAW - Original DSLR camera files. These must be processed to one of the above formats to be viewable and usable. These are also very large files and are primarily used by professional photographers.

Organizing Our Demo Folder

Here is a before screenshot of my Demo Folder. In keeping with a YYYY-MM system of naming folders, I have some work to do. I also need to sort the photos in the iPhone folders.

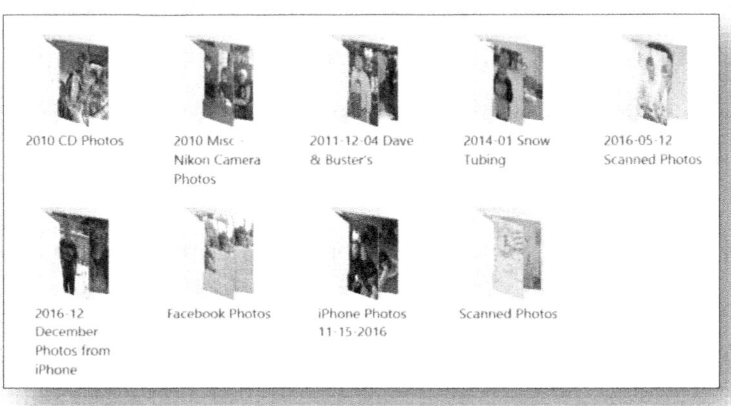

Because I will be organizing these photos by date, I do not need to save the location from where they came from. Here, I have done some of the necessary folder renaming.

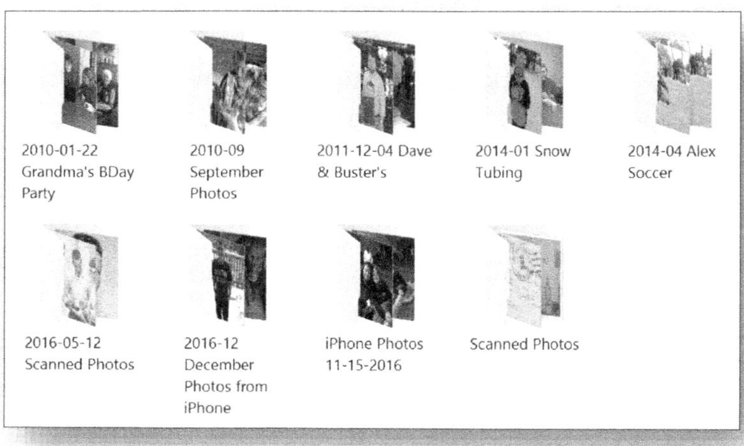

And here is the final screenshot of the organized folders in my Demo Folder.

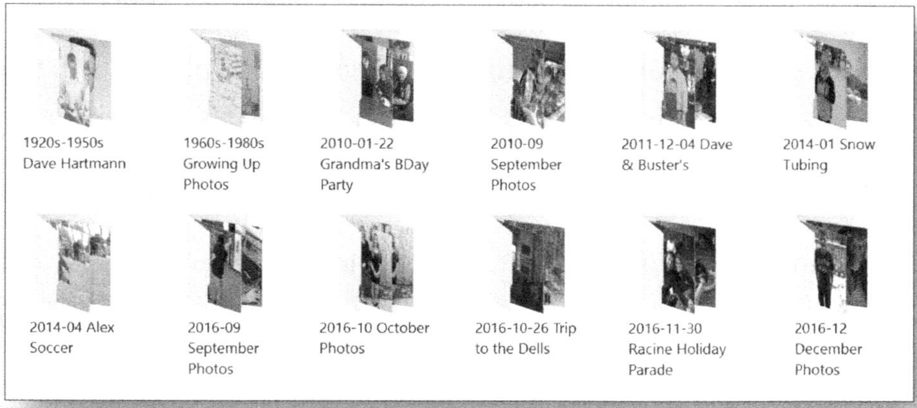

- Folders with scanned photos have been renamed to the date they were taken
- iPhone and DVD folders have been broken up into individual events or months of photos
- Folders are automatically sorted chronologically because of the YYYY-MM naming system.

Name	Type
1920s-1950s Dave Hartmann	File folder
1960s-1980s Growing Up Photos	File folder
2010-01-22 Grandma's BDay Party	File folder
2010-09 September Photos	File folder
2011-12-04 Dave & Buster's	File folder
2014-01 Snow Tubing	File folder
2014-04 Alex Soccer	File folder
2016-09 September Photos	File folder
2016-10 October Photos	File folder
2016-10-26 Trip to the Dells	File folder
2016-11-30 Racine Holiday Parade	File folder
2016-12 December Photos	File folder

Details View

Photo Organization Software Overview

We have now covered the general principals of organizing photos with File Explorer. Now, you may be interested in hearing about other options for sorting and saving your photos. Much of the work we did in File Explorer transfers over to the other programs out there.

In this section, we will give a quick overview of a few programs our clients use. Then, we'll talk about the programs we recommend for photo organization.

Picasa – I have bad news if this is your favorite program. Picasa is no longer is being supported by Google. People who use Picasa should be looking for a new solution to manage their photos. While some of our clients have been disappointed to hear this news, we do provide alternatives. For the most part, the newer software options do a much better job in helping consumers organize photos.

Google Drive & Google Photos – While these Google apps may help store smartphone photos temporarily, they should not be a long-term solution. Read the fine print of Google's User Agreement. You'll find that when you upload photos to their website, Google gathers an incredible amount of personal information and data to use and share with Google Analytics. We never recommend that our clients organize and store their photos with Google products.

Windows 10 Photos – This app comes with the Windows 10 operating system and replaces Windows Photo Gallery. We find this program to be clunky and difficult to use. It works in conjunction with OneDrive and can be very slow to load. We don't recommend this program for organizing photos, but you should be aware of it. It can be useful to edit photos occasionally. Here's a screenshot of how my Demo Folder folders look here.

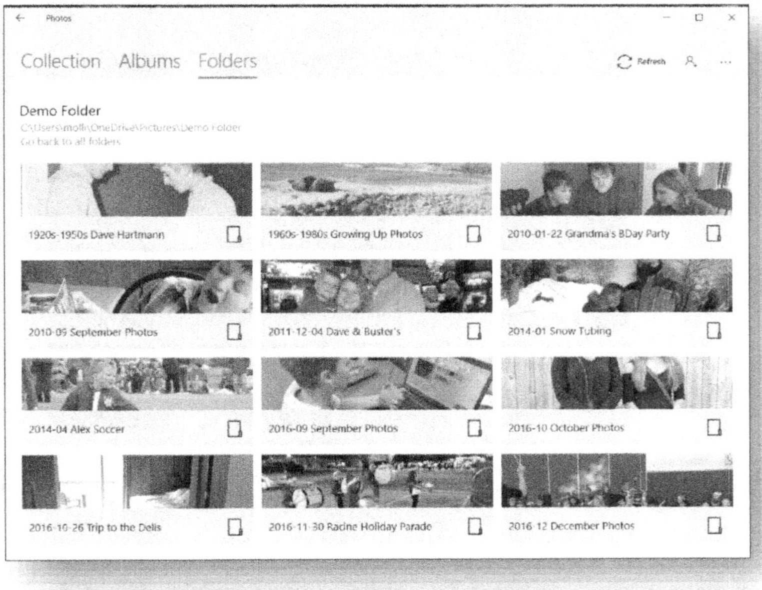

Once you click into a folder and open a picture, you have options to edit, share, etc.

Mylio - You can import your Pictures Folder into Mylio, and the program will maintain your folder structure. Visually, your photos and folders look wonderful. The editing features are more than adequate. You can connect an external hard drive for automatic backups. The basic version is free for now. Advanced users can purchase upgrades to Mylio. I have found that the basic version works great for people who are comfortable using File Explorer already and want to do more with their photos. See how my Demo Folders look in Mylio.

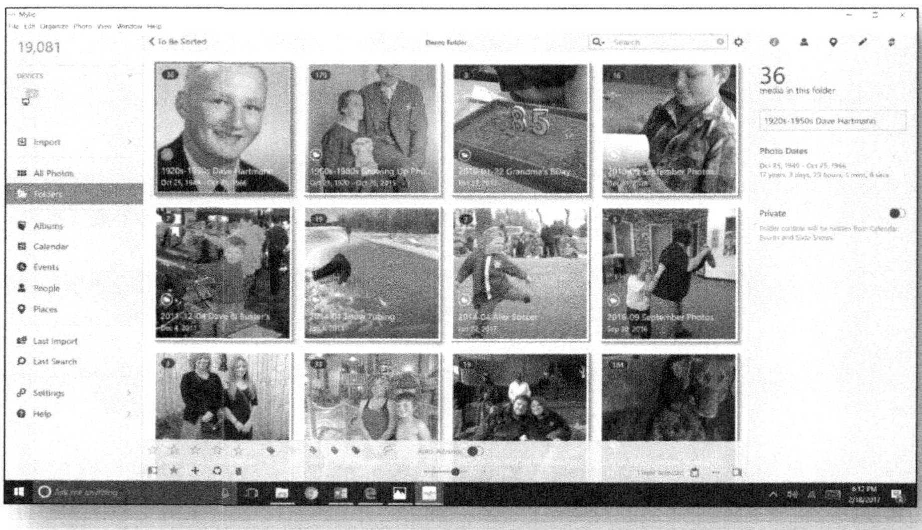

You can also see the left column resembles the File Explorer Navigation Pane. Mylio offers a robust calendar view as well as facial recognition. At a glance, you can see I have 19,081 photos in Mylio, my program of choice.

Forever Historian – This program offers a different look and feel to organizing your photos using vault technology. Facial recognition works well. Editing options include simple tasks from fixing red-eye all the way to cloning. It offers a timeline on the bottom where you can click on a date to see photos from that time. Forever Historian works together with Forever's photobook creation software, called Artisan. Forever also offers permanent online storage for photo backup.

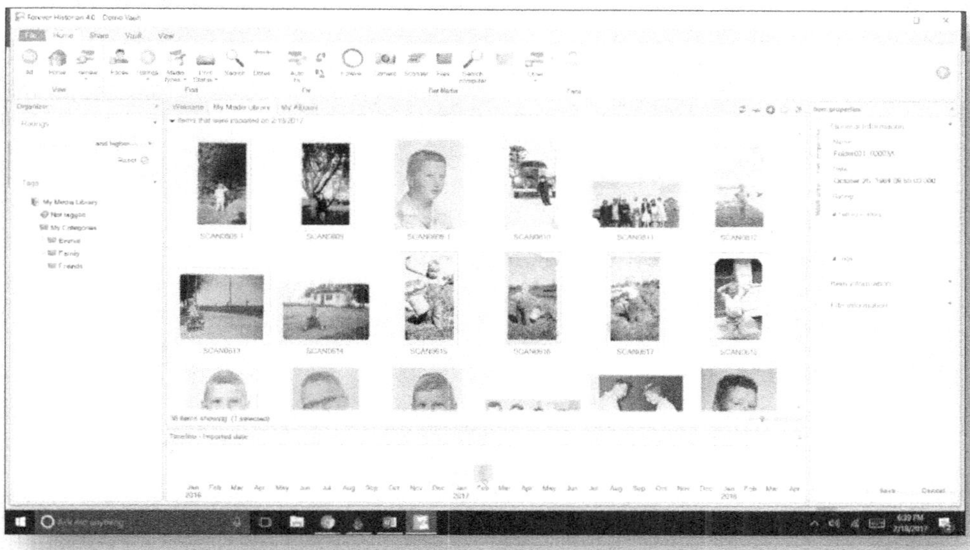

Organizing your photos takes time and patience to catch up on all the memories you have collected. These pictures do accumulate fast, so let's talk about what photos to delete next.

CHAPTER FIVE – DELETE AS YOU GO

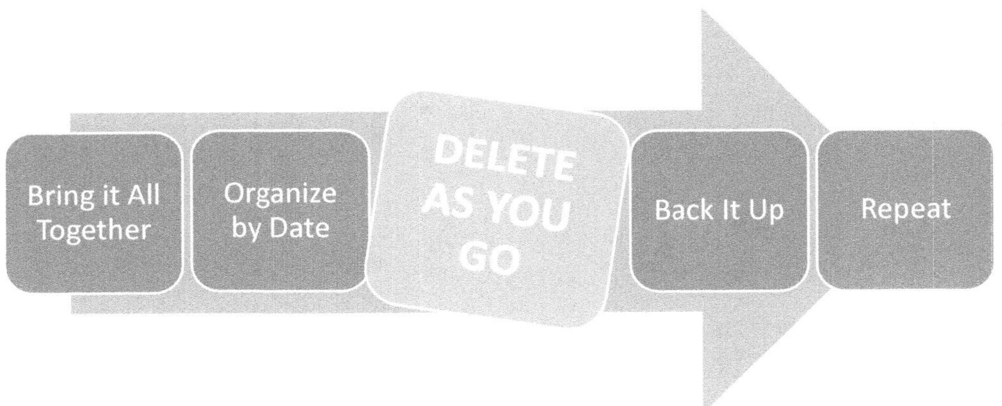

Now that you've had your fair share of computer and photo organizing education, let's chat about what pictures you should save.

And before we dive into that topic, we need to talk about something more pressing. . . What photos should you be taking? For some people, reducing the number of photos taken could be a game changer in how easy it is to save digital photos.

What Photos to Take

Today, it costs nothing to take a picture. In fact, we can set our cameras to take multiple pictures at one time. One of my clients, Mary, had set up her nice Nikon camera to do this. She was capturing something like 10 photos with one click. So at an afternoon birthday party for one of her children, she took around 50 pictures. Not bad, but now, multiply that by 10 each click and all of a sudden she had 500 photos. That's a lot to sort through and figure out what to print, which means. . . she never did anything with any of the photos.

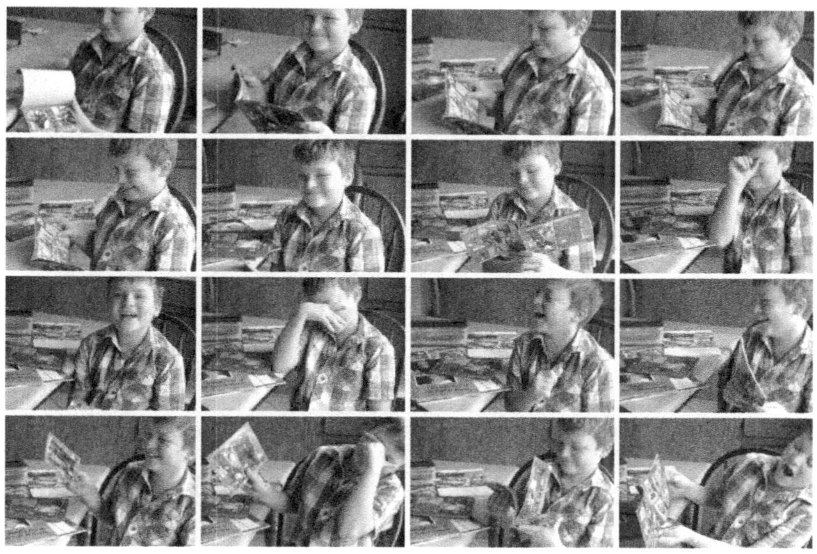

16 photos of the same moment. . .

It is truly okay to delete 15 of these!

In a different situation, one of our clients took over 2,000 photos while on amazing trip to Thailand. The seven-day trip was life changing. Yet she was frozen on where to start with creating a photobook of her experience.

I don't think our brains were made to process hundreds and thousands of moments caught on camera. So, when I talk with clients about their photo taking habits, we chat about:

- What photos they take
- What photos they truly need to tell their story

For any event, occasion or moment, you want to take just enough photos to:

1. Capture the moments and traditions you want to remember
2. Identify who was important in that moment

Then, it is time to put the camera away and enjoy. This is very hard for even me to do. My sister Rosie always used to say that taking too many photos can ruin the moment and having too many photos of an event tends to lessen the importance of any single photo from the event.

My client who used to take 500 pictures in an afternoon followed my advice. She has a much easier time managing her digital photos now.

Here's an example from Thanksgiving last year. Frying a turkey is a fun tradition for us. This past year, I took about 12 photos. See below which photos I have crossed out for deletion. For this event, I have captured the moment with my husband and children. We even got our family Christmas card photo out of the day!

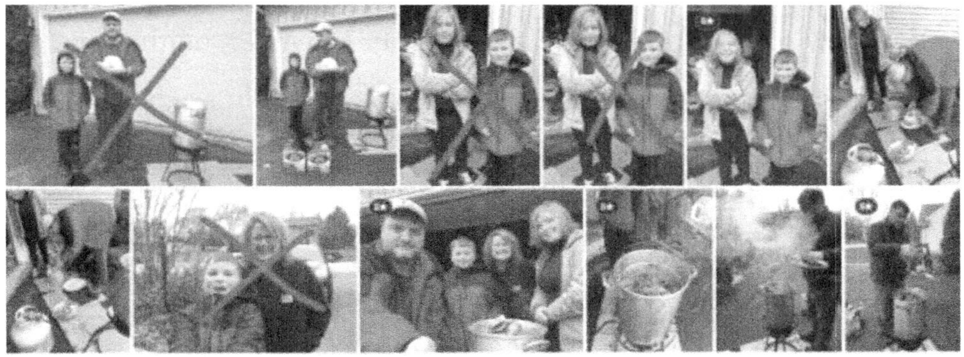

How Many Digital Photos Should You Keep?

So now that we have discussed what photos you should take, we can talk about what photos to keep.

I like to think about my photo collection in terms of how easy will it be for me to create a digital family yearbook or a photo calendar. No one wants to flip through thousands of photos when looking at family pictures. Imagine the following scenarios if you keep 250 photos a month:

- A family photobook for one year would have 3,000 photos. At six photos a page, that would be 500 pages. How long would that take to look through? Never mind that most inexpensive photobook options start with 20 pages.
- A slideshow playing those photos for three seconds each would last for two and a half hours.

You may have adorable children or pets; however, neither one of those situations sounds like the best way to reminisce.

Now, there's no saying that all the photos you keep need to go in the photobook or slideshow. I throw the numbers out there as a starting point. For my own digital photo collection, I aim to keep around 1,000 photos each year, give or take.

My ultimate goal is a family year photo book containing around 360 of my best photos from one year. This comes to roughly 30 per month depending on events and holidays.

My Personal Family Photo Collection Formula

Save 80 to 100 Photos Per Month
Around 1,000 photos per year

Star 30 per month
360 total per year

Amazing family photo book/slideshow

Family photo calendar

Each year, I keep around 1,000 photos. When I go into my photos monthly, I track my progress and see how many photos I have. 1,000 is just a rough number; some years I save 1,100 and some years I have between 850 and 950.

The next tier of the pyramid is the most important. Of the photos I save in a year, I mark or "star" around 360 photos, which are my favorite pictures. These are the photos I would be upset to lose.

By starring your best photos, you are acting as a "curator" of your photo collection. These are the photos that make up my photobooks, photo gifts and more. Also, these are the ones that I want to pass on to my children and future generations. By starring these photos, I have a much easier time making my photo projects since I don't have to search for the best photos.

In Windows File Explorer, select the photo you wish to star and then select five stars in the Detail pane. I don't worry about how many stars each photo should get; that would be too time consuming. I simply five-star my favorites. Be sure to click Save at the bottom of the Detail pane.

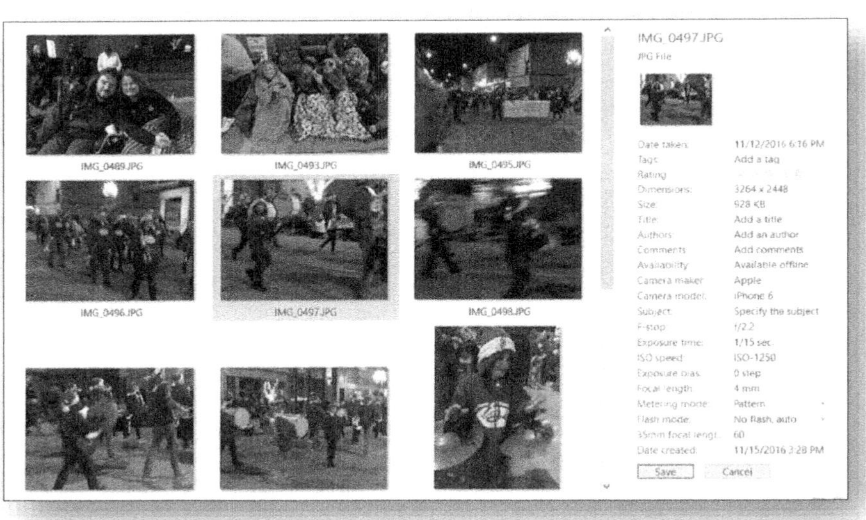

Unfortunately, Windows File Explorer makes it difficult to find your five star photos. On the next page, I have included a screenshot of File Explorer in the Details view. By right-clicking on the Column title bar, I added the Rating to my Details view. Then, click on the Rating column to sort your photos by rating.

Pictures > Demo Folder > 2016-11-30 Racine Holiday Parade

Name	Date	Type	Size	Rating
IMG_0489.JPG	11/12/2016 5:41 PM	JPG File	1,382 KB	☆☆☆☆☆
IMG_0493.JPG	11/12/2016 5:48 PM	JPG File	1,849 KB	☆☆☆☆☆
IMG_0495.JPG	11/12/2016 6:16 PM	JPG File	838 KB	☆☆☆☆☆
IMG_0496.JPG	11/12/2016 6:16 PM	JPG File	926 KB	☆☆☆☆☆
IMG_0497.JPG	11/12/2016 6:16 PM	JPG File	929 KB	☆☆☆☆☆
IMG_0498.JPG	11/12/2016 6:16 PM	JPG File	816 KB	☆☆☆☆☆
IMG_0499.JPG	11/12/2016 6:16 PM	JPG File	1,020 KB	☆☆☆☆☆
IMG_0500.JPG	11/12/2016 6:16 PM	JPG File	990 KB	☆☆☆☆☆
IMG_0503.JPG	11/12/2016 6:20 PM	JPG File	1,594 KB	☆☆☆☆☆
IMG_0504.JPG	11/12/2016 6:20 PM	JPG File	1,548 KB	☆☆☆☆☆
IMG_0505.JPG	11/12/2016 6:20 PM	JPG File	1,467 KB	☆☆☆☆☆
IMG_0509.JPG	11/14/2016 12:20 AM	JPG File	243 KB	☆☆☆☆☆
IMG_0510.JPG	11/14/2016 12:21 AM	JPG File	201 KB	☆☆☆☆☆
IMG_0511.JPG	11/14/2016 12:21 AM	JPG File	201 KB	☆☆☆☆☆

Size All Columns to Fit
✓ Name
✓ Date
✓ Type
✓ Size
Tags
Date created
Date modified
Date taken
Dimensions
✓ Rating
More...

For those who are comfortable with customizing their File Explorer windows, there is an excellent online resource called the How-To Geek by Walter Glenn. Photo organizer, Carolyn Burnham recommends his article called *"How to Customize Folder Views with Windows' Five Te mplates."* You can find this article by searching for the title online.

If you looking to rate your photos and to easily find your favorites, we recommend using a photo organization software such as Mylio or Forever Historian.

Back to our pyramid . . .

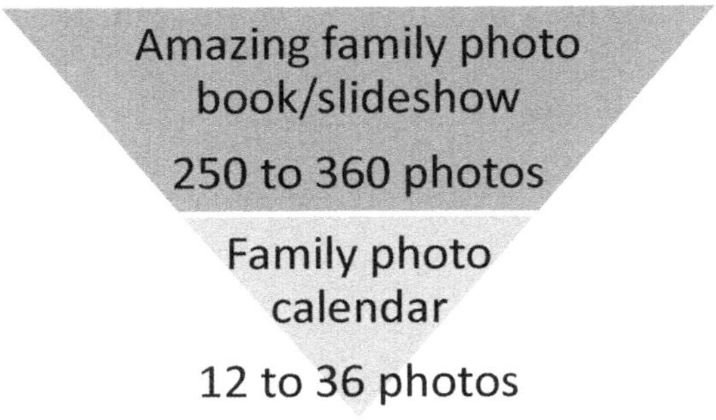

Amazing family photo book/slideshow

250 to 360 photos

Family photo calendar

12 to 36 photos

Look at the last two tiers of the pyramid. By organizing and saving your favorite photos, photo books and calendars become much easier. Imagine being the hit of the family party when you bring printed family photos along!

What Our Digital Photo Clients Have

At Pixologie, our digital photo clients have between 12,000 and 40,000 digital photos. My own collection includes 19,000 photos covering from the early 1900s to the present. This includes the scanned copies of printed photos.

Think about this . . . Do our children and grandchildren want to have this many digital photos passed down to them someday? No way!

It's time to delete some more!

What Digital Photos Should You Delete?

For some of you, deleting a photo may be a big deal. You may feel like you are somehow harming the memory or lessening the feelings of the moment. Let it go and start deleting!

Our first rule is if you love the photo (whether it's not the best, blurry, etc.), then save it by all means! ***You just can't feel that way about every photo.***

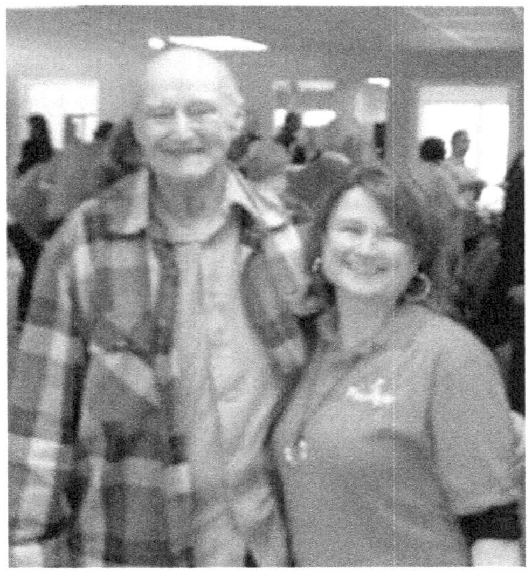

This picture is of my dad and me when Pixologie had its grand opening. It's blurred and not the best photo, but I love it. And my dad is gone now, so this picture is priceless to me.

Here are my tips on what pictures you should delete. These tips are similar to what we have recommended when sorting printed photos. Delete photos that:

- Have no identifiable people and the setting is represented in other pictures from that moment (example: landscape photos from a vacation; birthday party photos with none of your family in the pictures)

- Are repetitive in nature (example: zoo photos of the animals or crowds; cute baby photos with a dozen different expressions; pet snapshots in various locations around the house)
- Show unflattering angles and expressions (example: nearly all selfies, any picture that might be embarrassing in a bad way or would be mean to share)
- Don't add anything new to the memory (example: vacation photos of destination or tourist stops from every angle; graduation photos where your child is seen in six different places in line to receive diploma)

On the next page, I have a grid of photos from a day my daughter Hannah had sailing lessons. My son Alex was having fun with a Pirates of the Caribbean sword while we waited for her to finish. I crossed out photos I will delete.

- Some of the photos are repetitive
- Some don't have my daughter in them
- Some don't add anything new to what we remember about the day

You may choose different criteria to delete some of your photos. The important part of this process is that you become okay with deleting photos that aren't necessary to tell the story of that moment.

Another Example

Can you see the first two pictures in the middle row look similar? I just couldn't decide which one to delete so I kept them both. I am guilty too!

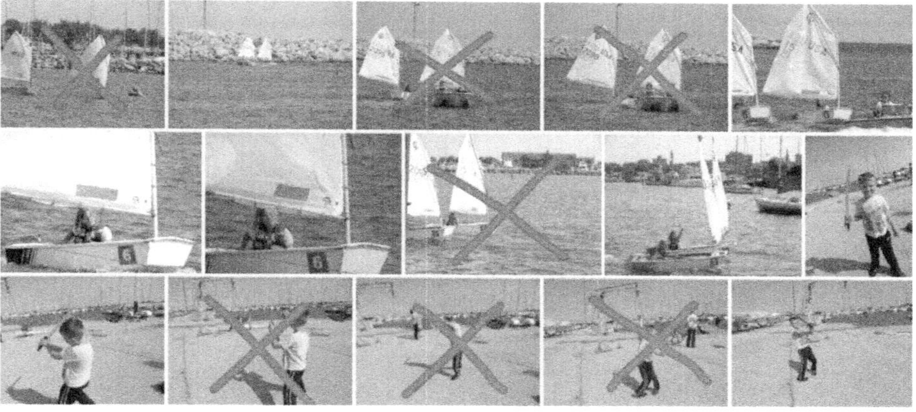

Hopefully, this chapter has given you some insight on what photos to take, keep and delete!

CHAPTER SIX – BACKING UP YOUR PHOTOS

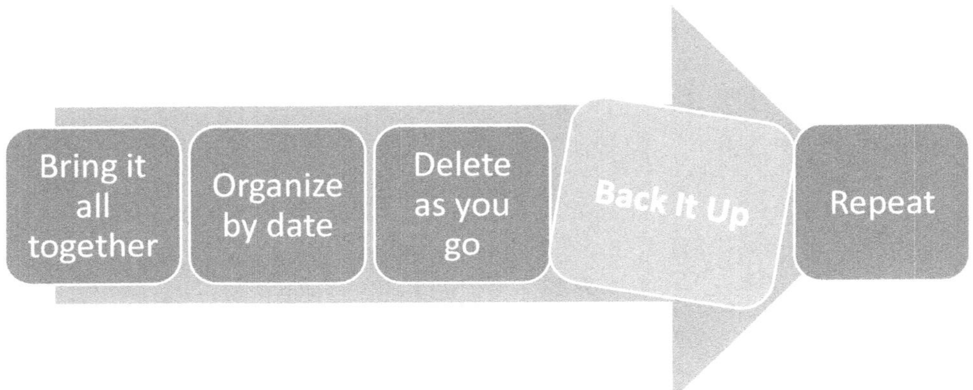

So now you have photos organized in your Pictures folder. No matter where you are with organizing your digital photos, backing up routinely is important. We recommend your Pictures folder be backed up in two locations.

FIRST COPY - Copy your Pictures folder to an external hard drive. Remember to back up on the external hard drive every time you add photos to your Pictures folder. If you are using software like Mylio or Forever Historian, you can connect an external hard drive and the programs will automatically back up your work.

SECOND COPY – Should be stored outside of your home. In the event of a fire, burglary or other disaster, this copy could be important. Options include a second external hard drive stored in safe deposit box or a cloud-based backup.

Backing Up to an External Hard Drive

We have provided a description of external hard drives already. For your photo backup, clearly label your external hard drive. Always use the same drive for backup purposes. You can manually back up your Pictures folder to your external hard drive.

Windows 10 does come with an automatic backup feature. This requires keeping an external hard drive connected to your computer. Windows will automatically back up your files to it as long as the drive is connected.

Keep in mind that running an external hard drive constantly may shorten its life span. As long as you have two backups of your Pictures, you will be covered if something should happen to one external hard drive.

Here's how to turn on automatic backup:

Go to Settings-Update & Security-Backup. Turn on Automatically back up my files, then click on More options.

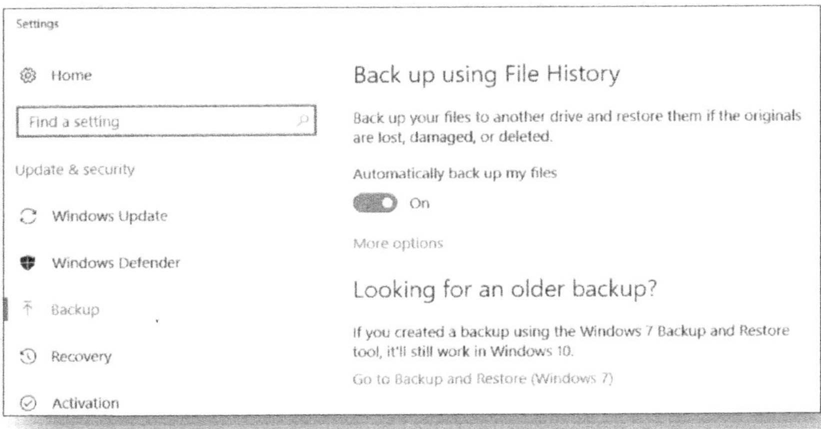

Here you can set when you want the computer to back up and how long you'd like the backups to be saved. Scroll down to make sure your Pictures Folder is on the list to be backed up.

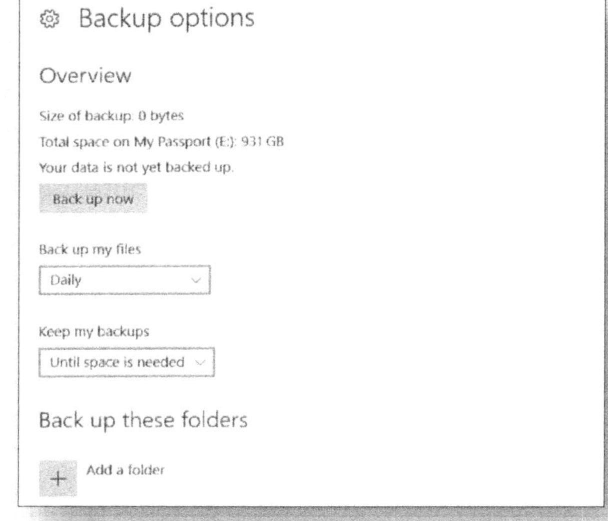

For your second backup, you can have a second external hard drive. Or there are cloud options to consider.

Understanding the Cloud

For many of us, the cloud sounds like something vague, techy and way out there. Consumers are mistrustful of the cloud for privacy and security reasons. Also, many just don't understand what the cloud is. Let's start off with a basic definition of the cloud.

The cloud, simply, refers to software and services that run on the internet instead of your computer. Recognize these?

From email to entertainment to office work, the sky is the limit for what you can do online in the cloud. However, more often, when people think of the cloud, they are thinking of what might be stored in the cloud. This refers to one area of services that is offered.

Cloud-Based Storage – The websites that are dedicated to storing files online vary in how they work. Generally, we recommend you stay away from the free storage sites. However, there are many reputable, paid cloud storage sites. They include:

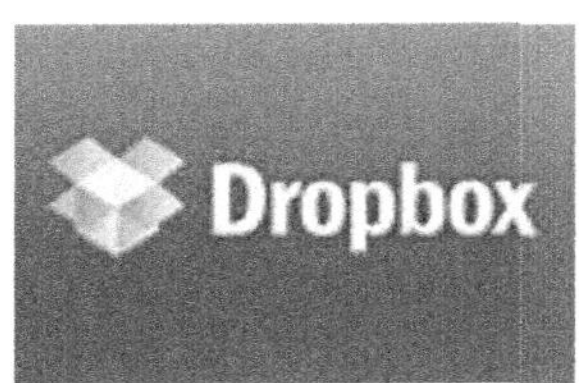

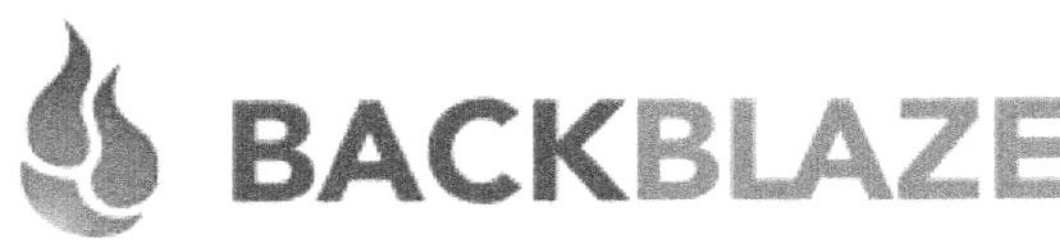

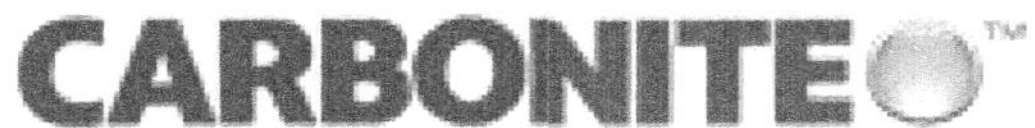

Dropbox, Backblaze and Carbonite would make a good second backup place for your photos. Backup services run around $50 to $100 per year.

We primarily recommend iCloud for those who use Mac computers. (Interesting note: if you have an iPhone, you automatically have an iCloud account. Login at icloud.com using your Apple ID and password.)

Cloud-Based Photo Storage – There are cloud services that specifically deal with photos. This includes internet sites where you can order photobooks, calendars and prints. These are the companies we worry about, as many have come and gone. Remember Picasa? We encourage people to make sure they have all their original photos on their computer. Below are examples of services that currently exist.

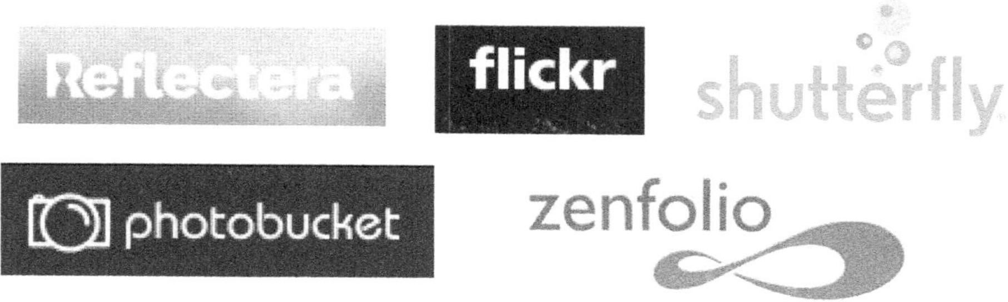

Permanent Cloud Photo Storage - Five years ago, this concept didn't even exist. Today, Forever is the first and only company to offer permanent cloud-based storage.

At Pixologie, we have watched Forever since they first launched permanent storage in 2014. They listened to feedback from photo organizers around the country. They continue to improve the functionality of their cloud-based storage. A portion of the cost of storage is put aside into the Forever Fund. Users can feel secure knowing their photos will be migrated to future technology.

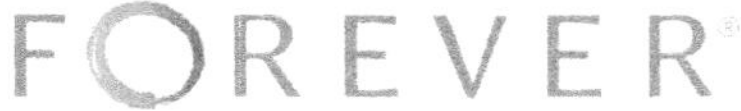

In full disclosure, Pixologie sells Forever Storage along with other products. We think Forever is an excellent option for backing up the best of your photos. It is a tool that will help consumers pass their photos and stories to future generations.

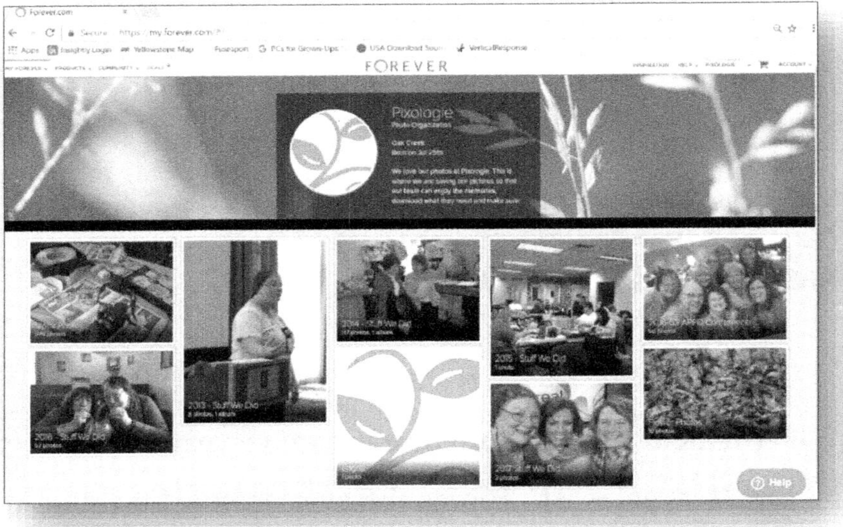

Above is a screenshot of the home screen of Pixologie's Forever Account. You can see a simple view of the albums we have created.

Here you can check out our full library and some of the additional features Forever offers. By clicking on a photo, users can access simple editing tools as well.

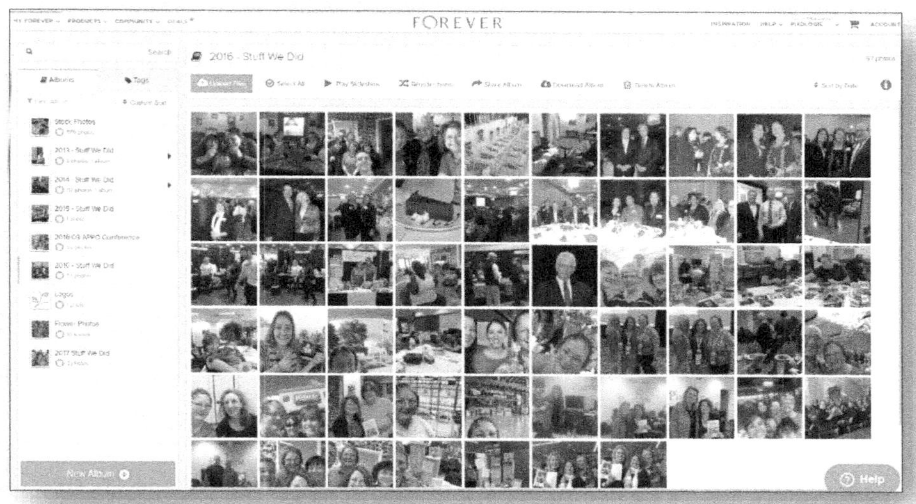

Even with Forever, we recommend that people store their original photos on their computer. They should also have an additional backup on an external hard drive. The best case scenario is to create a Family Year photo book so that you also have a print copy of your best family photos.

So, we have now covered backing up your photos with a variety of options. You'll need to determine which two methods will work best for you. The next and final step in our system is Repeat!

CHAPTER SEVEN – REPEAT

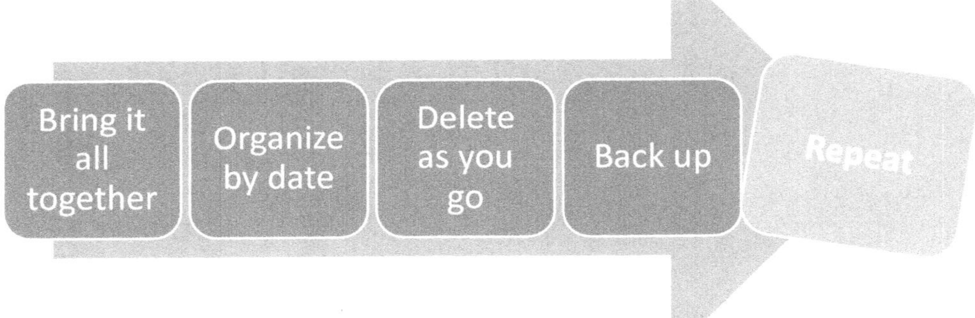

Are you committed to saving your family photos for years to come? If yes, then you are going to want to return each month at least to save your latest digital photos. Here's a few benefits of repeating the process routinely:

- You'll get faster at saving your photos because of the repetition
- You'll be more comfortable deleting pictures with less thought process

- You'll be able to create photo books and calendars at the end of the year
- You'll be more thoughtful in what photos you take

Last year, I was speaking to a church friend about her pictures. She mentioned, "I know I really need to get some of my photos printed from my phone." What's more important? Getting that photo printed or saving into your family photo collection?

There are apps that can get prints made direct from a phone, which is great. However, if we don't save the photos in one place and back them up, those memories are in danger of being lost. I have personal experience with losing important photos. A few years back, my phone was stolen. Three weeks of photos not backed up included pictures from a very special trip.

Don't wait until you've lost a phone or had a computer crash. Do something about your digital photo mess today. We've heard from many people after it is too late. We can't stress enough how important it is that you continue to organize and save your digital photos.

Photo projects can then become a routine part of your life. Often, I meet people who can't even think about making a photo book. They have no idea where to start or to find the digital photos they'd want to be in a book.

Today, you can be one of the people who have organized their photos successfully. Take the steps we have outlined in this book. Commit to working on your photos monthly.

Your family can have a photo book printed to celebrate memories from years ago or from new memories made today. We wish you the best in your photo organization and preservation journey.

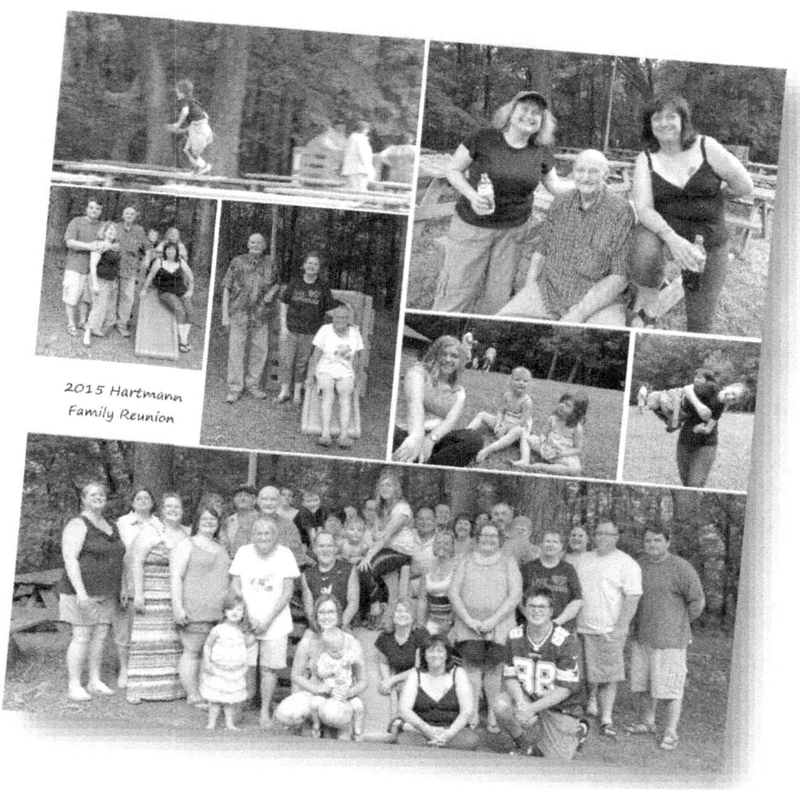

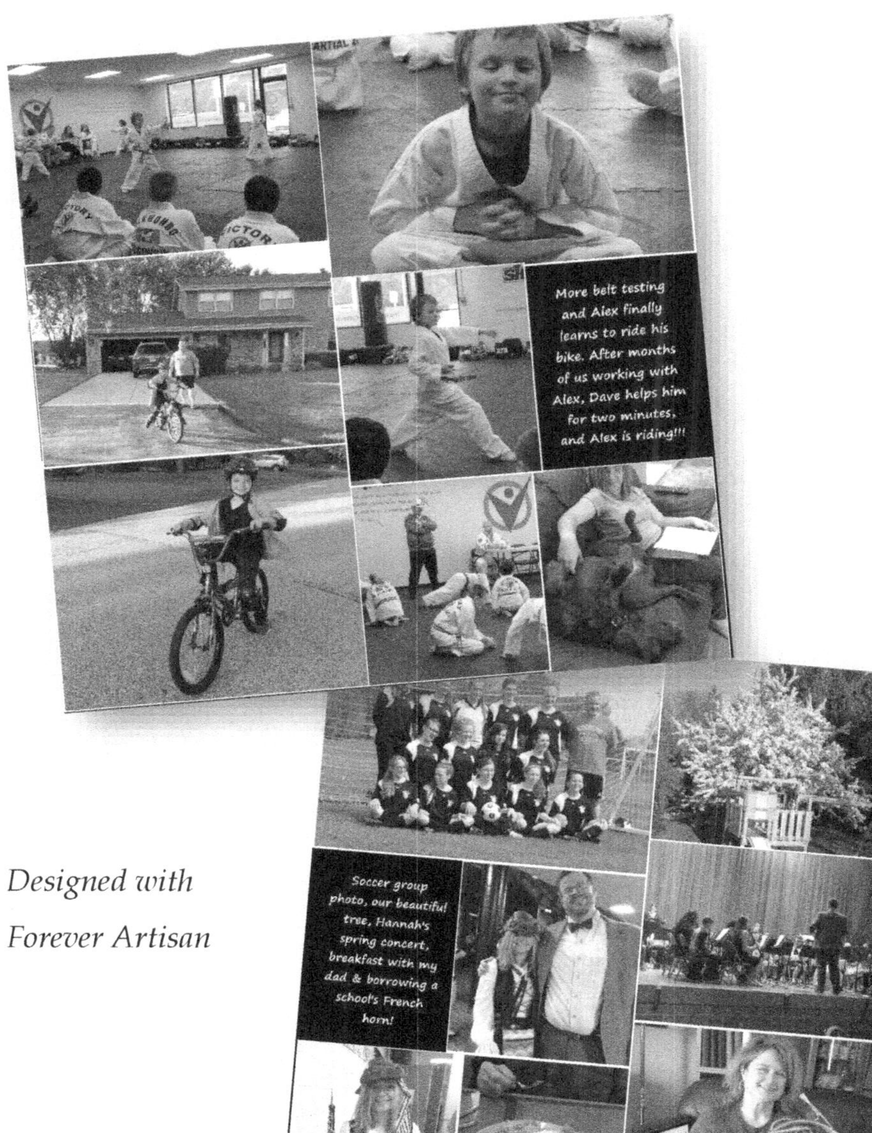

Designed with Forever Artisan

CHAPTER EIGHT – IF ALL ELSE FAILS

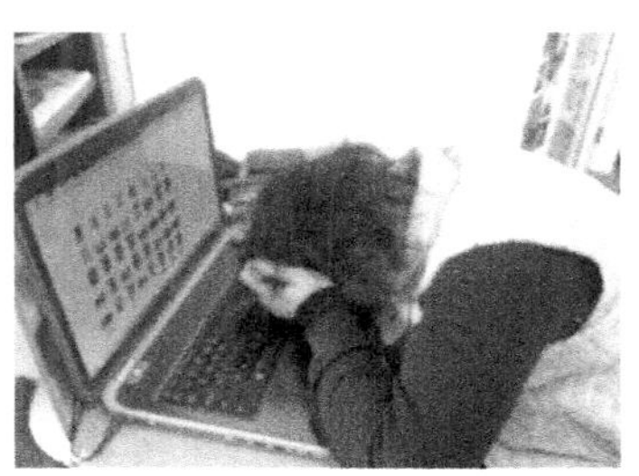

After reading through this book, does the thought of organizing your digital photos still overwhelm you? That's okay. You can hire someone to organize your digital photos for you.

We love to help people organize their own photos either at their home, in our studio, over the phone with remote assistance or with another Pixologie owner.

Another great resource if you don't have a Pixologie in your area is the Association of Personal Photo Organizers. On their website, you will find resources and a directory of personal photo organizers around the country. When you hire someone to help you with your photo projects, we recommend asking for two references. If you are using an online scanning service, please Google their name and read their reviews.

APPENDIX A – DROPBOX & ONEDRIVE

Dropbox and Microsoft OneDrive are two services that offer online backup of your files. They also offer file syncing between computers. Often, I find my clients have these installed on their PC, but they are not sure what they are or how they work. (Google Drive is also an online backup and file-syncing service. Due to its User Agreement requirements, we don't recommend it.)

Let's define backing up versus file syncing.

Backing up - provides a copy of files from one device or location (computer, external hard drive, online cloud storage) to another.

File syncing - ensures files match from one device (computer, tablets, smartphones, etc) to another. Sometimes, file syncing results in a backup. However, when deleting a file from one location, it will be deleted on all other devices.

Dropbox – Many people use Dropbox to share photos with their colleagues, friends and family. They usually send an email invitation to view the folders. The person who is invited receives the email and may create an account to view the photos. They also may have downloaded and installed the app to their computer. If Dropbox has been installed on your computer, you'll see it in your File Explorer. Although it has a symbol of a blue box, Dropbox acts just like another folder on your computer. Original files are stored on your computer, with a copy saved in your account at Dropbox.com.

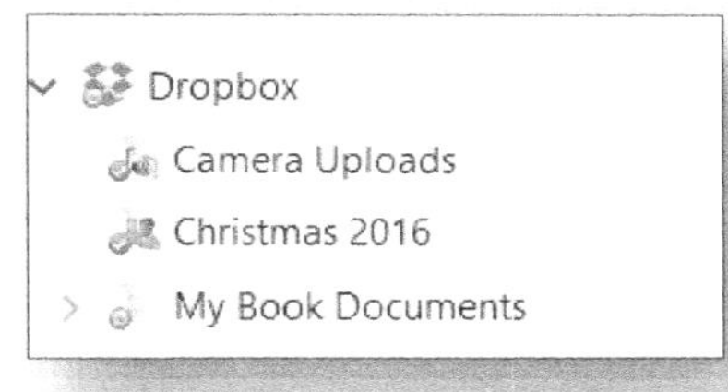

You may see a dialog box appear every time you connect a device to your computer that contains photos. It looks like this:

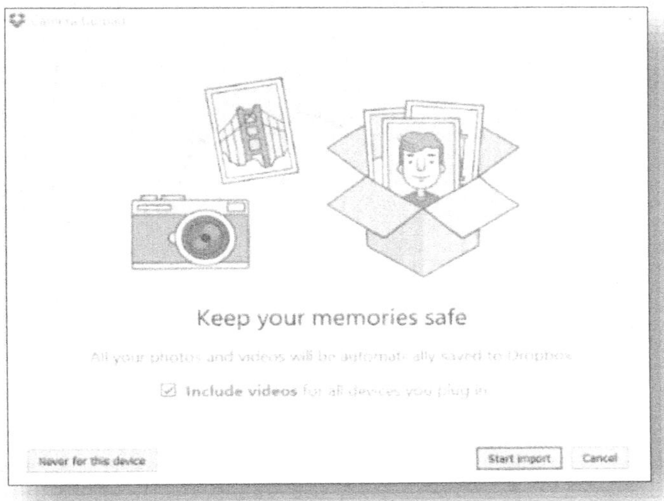

When you click Start import, the photos are copied to your Dropbox/Camera Uploads folder. You may find this a handy feature. Or. . . you can turn Dropbox off so it doesn't ask you this every time you connect your phone.

Under System Settings, click on Devices and then AutoPlay. Or. . . you can search in your task bar for AutoPlay to get this screen.

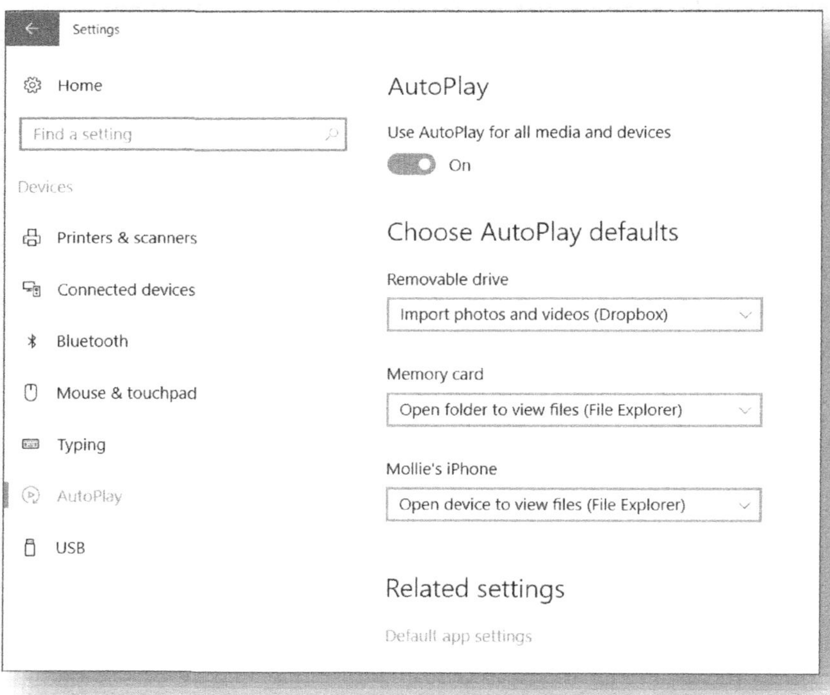

Turn AutoPlay off or choose settings for each type of device. When you click on one of the options, a dropdown menu will appear. You can see that there are several options depending upon what is installed on your computer. The options here include Photos, OneDrive and Dropbox, among others.

I like to choose "Open device to view files (File Explorer)" so that I can view my photos in File Explorer.

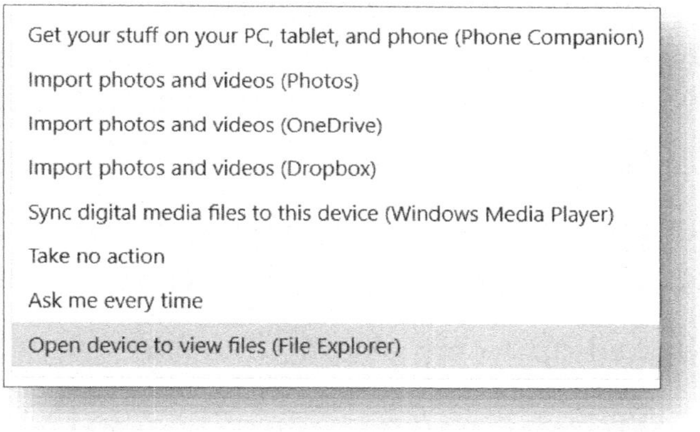

Get your stuff on your PC, tablet, and phone (Phone Companion)
Import photos and videos (Photos)
Import photos and videos (OneDrive)
Import photos and videos (Dropbox)
Sync digital media files to this device (Windows Media Player)
Take no action
Ask me every time
Open device to view files (File Explorer)

Dropbox can be very useful for people who like to share documents and photos. For people who use multiple computers, Dropbox can sync files between the two computers. For the purposes of photo organization, we do not like to rely on this as a backup solution.

Microsoft OneDrive - Microsoft has offered online storage for many years under several different names. Currently called OneDrive, it comes installed on all new Windows 10 computers. It also functions like Dropbox. Original files are stored on your computer in the OneDrive folder. A copy is stored in your Microsoft account at OneDrive.com.

People who subscribe to Office 365 receive 1TB of storage space at OneDrive.com. This could be enough to back up everything on your computer.

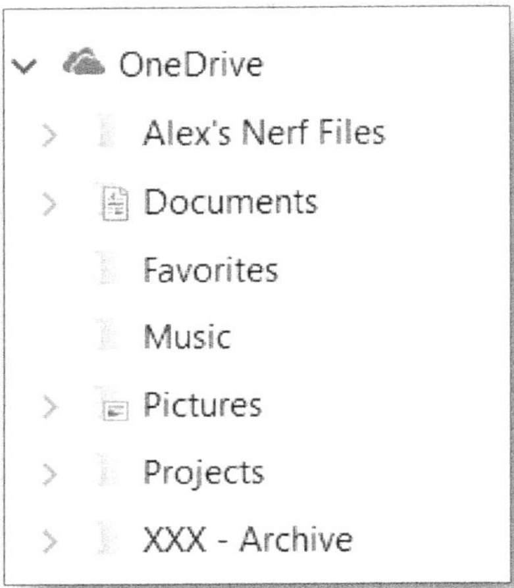

Look at the screenshot from my Navigation Pane to the right. You can see the folders that I have stored in my OneDrive folder (designated with the cloud). These files are being backed up to my OneDrive online account.

OneDrive
Alex's Nerf Files
Documents
Favorites
Music
Pictures
Projects
XXX - Archive

Occasionally, I have had clients whose photos automatically go into their OneDrive/Pictures folder. This can be confusing if you have photos saved elsewhere. To turn off this feature, follow the instructions from the previous pages for Dropbox.

APPENDIX B – WINDOWS EXPLORER

Throughout this book, I have used screenshots from Windows 10 File Explorer. For people using computers with the Windows 7 operating system, the look of Windows Explorer is somewhat different. I have added a few screenshots here to point out the important features of Windows Explorer. Please note that many of the principles of working with Windows Explorer will be similar as described in Chapter Two.

Below, you can see the Windows Explorer looks like a stack of file folders. Double-click on this to open Windows Explorer and see your folders.

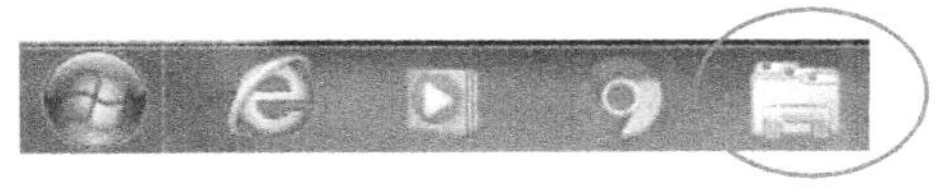

Basic View of Windows Explorer

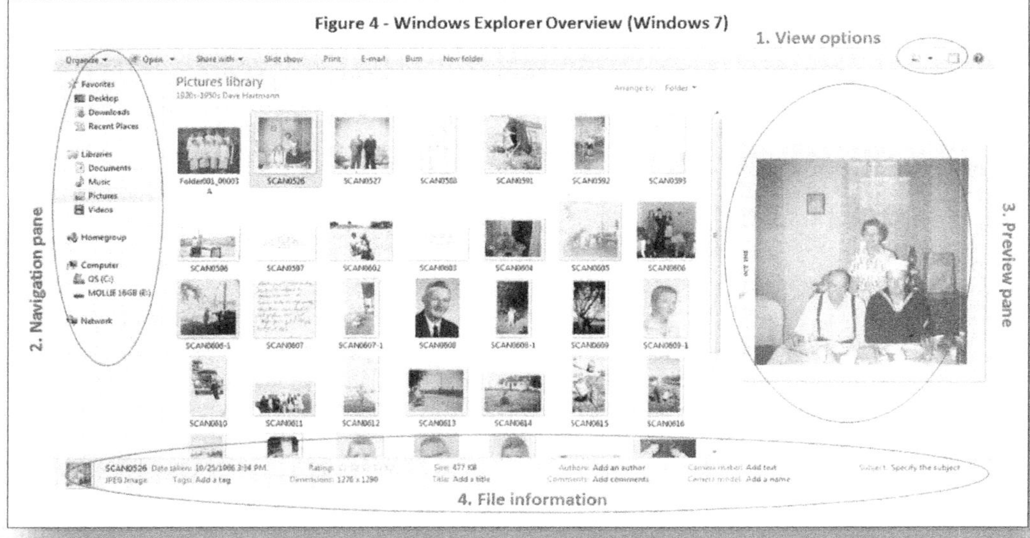

Figure 4 - Windows Explorer Overview (Windows 7)

1. View options - Click on the triangle next to the photo icon to choose how to view your photos (small icons, details, etc.) Click on the icon next to the question mark to open or close the Preview pane.
2. Navigation pane - View the folders on your computer and the devices connected to your computer.
3. Preview pane - See a preview of the selected file
4. File information - See the details of the photo you have selected

Adding New Folders

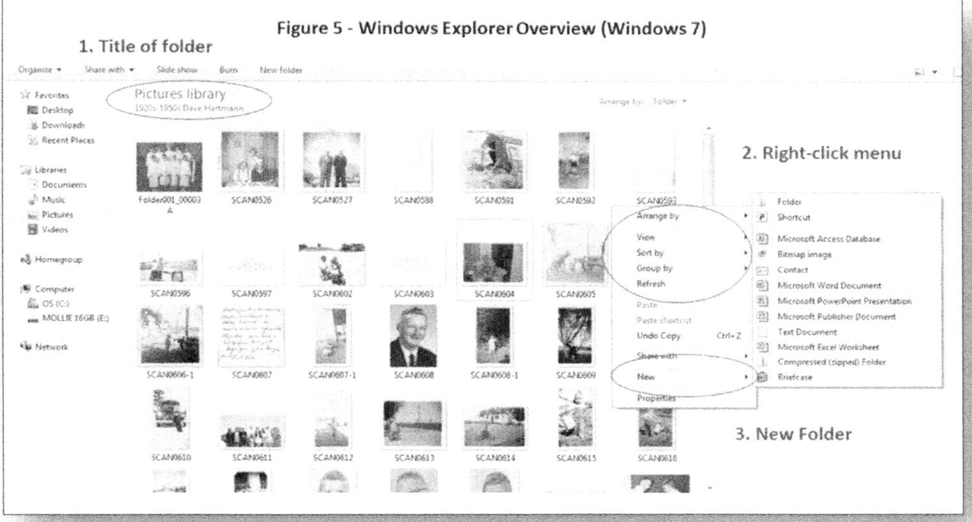

Figure 5 - Windows Explorer Overview (Windows 7)

1. Title of folder - Displays the folder name. Here, we are in a folder named 1920s-1950s David Hartmann which is located in the Pictures library (or Pictures folder)
2. Right-click on a blank area of the window to get a menu of options. Change your view, sort order and more in this menu.
3. Select New and an additional menu will pop out. Create a New Folder if needed.

Using Multiple Windows

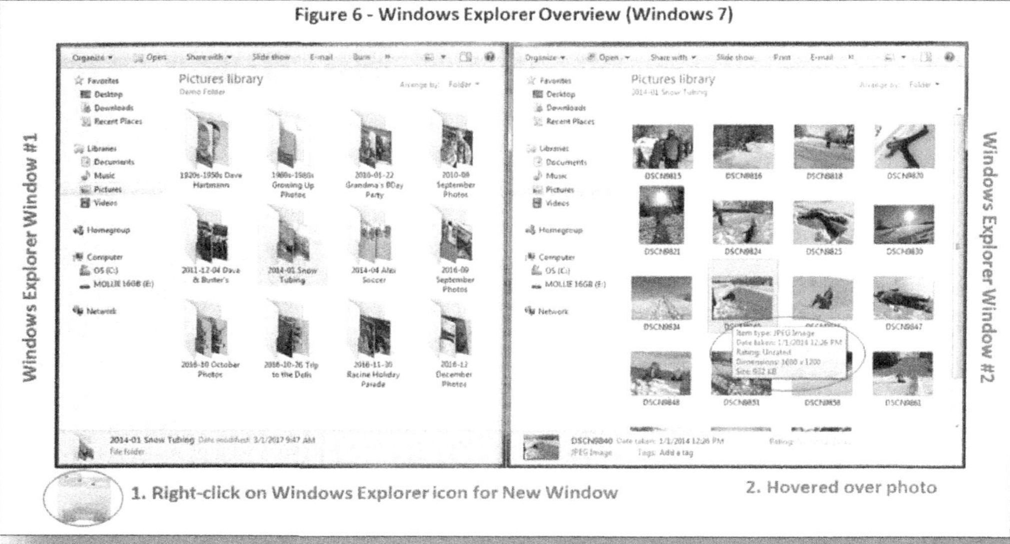

Figure 6 - Windows Explorer Overview (Windows 7)

Here we have added an additional window to our view. Assuming you already have one Windows Explorer window visible, next you will:

1. Right-click on the Windows Explorer icon – A menu will appear. Simply click on Windows Explorer to have a new window appear. Resize your windows as needed to have both displayed.
2. Hovered over photo – See photo information

With two windows open, you can easily move photos to your Pictures folder. Chapter Two will be worth a second look for people who are using Windows Explorer to organize photos.

APPENDIX C – ABOUT PIXOLOGIE

Pixologie is a photo and media organization and management company. Mollie Bartelt and Ann Matuszak started the company because they love photos and the stories that are captured in them. They believe that relationships and lives can be improved when individuals and families celebrate their memories and traditions by looking through their photos together.

Bringing a wealth of non-profit business management, direct sales and social service experience, Ann and Mollie believe photo and media organization services offers individuals, families and even organizations and businesses a place to start and the tools to preserve their photos.

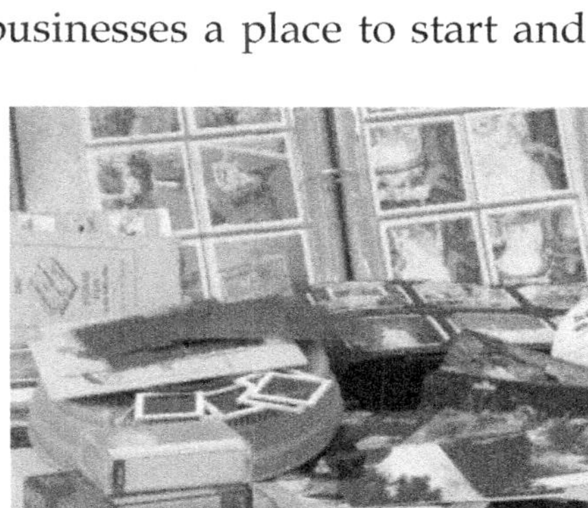

Pixologie, Inc. is located in the greater Milwaukee, Wisconsin area and is unique in offering photo organization and management services, onsite do-it-yourself options for our clients and trademark licensing for entrepreneurs.

Please contact us for more information. We would love to be a resource for you in your photo and media projects!

Mollie Bartelt – mollieb@pixologieinc.com

Ann Matuszak (Licensing) – annm@pixologieinc.com

Website: www.pixologieinc.com

Phone: 414-731-1881

Address: 9803 S. 13th Street, Oak Creek, WI 53154

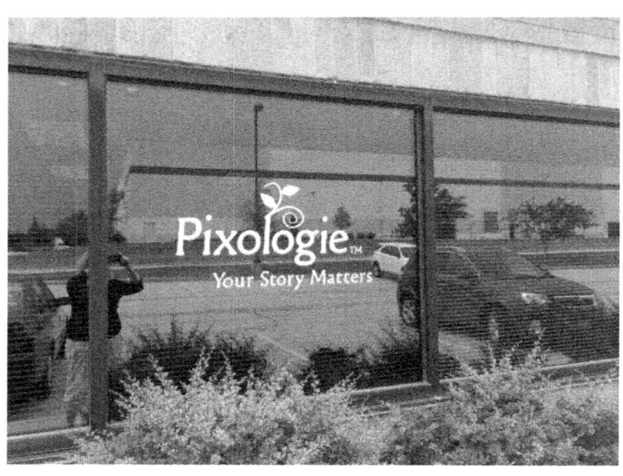

RESOURCES

Pixologie – A Photo Organization Company
www.pixologieinc.com
Telephone: 414-731-1881
Email: contact@pixologieinc.com

The Association of Personal Photo Organizers
www.appo.com
Find a photo organizer near you

E-Z Photo Scan
www.ezphotoscan.com
Telephone: 866-562-4660
Email: info@ezphotoscan.com
For high speed scanning resources

Forever
www.forever.com
For permanent storage, Forever Historian and Forever Artisan

Mylio
www.mylio.com
For photo organization and editing software

Made in the USA
Las Vegas, NV
05 August 2022